Ready-to-Use Activities for Teaching MACBETH

JOHN WILSON SWOPE

THE CENTER FOR APPLIED
RESEARCH IN EDUCATION
West Nyack, New York 10995

Dedication

To my most influential teachers:
my students, past and present.

10 9 8 7 6 5 4 3 2 1

Library of Congress Cataloging-in-Publication Data

Swope, John Wilson.
    Ready-to-use activities for teaching Macbeth / by John Wilson
Swope.
        p.   cm. — (Shakespeare teacher's activities library)
    Includes bibliographical references.
    ISBN 0–87628–115–3
    1. Shakespeare, William, 1564–1616. Macbeth.   2. Shakespeare,
William, 1564–1616—Study and teaching—Aids and devices.
3. Macbeth, King of Scotland, 11th cent.—In literature.
4. Activity programs in education.   5. Drama in education.
I. Title. II. Series: Swope, John Wilson. Shakespeare teacher's
activities library.
PR2823.S96   1994
822.3'3—dc20   93–46124
                                                CIP

ISBN 0-87628-115-3

**The Center for Applied Research
in Education,** Professional Publishing
West Nyack, New York 10995
Simon & Schuster, A Paramount Communications Company

Printed in the United States of America

About This Resource

Shakespeare's *Macbeth,* like *Romeo and Juliet, Julius Caesar,* and *Hamlet,* is a common choice for literature programs. As teachers, we enjoy these works and think them important for more than their stories. For me, Shakespeare's ability to observe human nature and convey it through language commands my attention. His characters act and interact with others in ways that I recognize around me. His poetry conveys human experience through a timeless literary form.

Although we prize Shakespeare's plays, they present many problems for our students as first-time readers. As teachers, we want our students to comprehend the plot, understand the motives of the characters, appreciate the language, and decipher countless allusions—sometimes after only a single reading.

Before most students study *Macbeth,* they have already studied either *Romeo and Juliet* or *Julius Caesar.* Even with this previous exposure to Shakespeare's plays, the students often expect to have problems with the Elizabethan language and conventions of blank verse; however, they possess knowledge and personal experience to help them understand and appreciate the play. Teenage readers can identify with many of the situations, characters, and themes within Shakespeare's *Macbeth.* Students can identify persons who abuse power or whose faces betray their actions as Macbeth does. As teenagers, they know firsthand about struggles for power and autonomy. They are also all too familiar with peers who, like Lady Macbeth, threaten, cajole, plead, or shame them into actions or situations they might not otherwise encounter. When we help students recall, organize, and share their relevant knowledge and experience, it becomes a valuable resource for them to begin understanding, appreciating, and interpreting the play.

As with other volumes in *Shakespeare Teacher's Activities Library, Ready-to-Use Activities for Teaching Macbeth* is a collection of student-centered activities for presenting the play to first-time readers. I've designed these activities to help students recall prior knowledge and personal experience that they can relate to the play. When students have little prior knowledge or experience that they can relate to the play, I have designed activities such as the *plot summaries, scenarios for improvisation,* and *prereading vocabulary* to help create their knowledge.

Although students expect structure in a classroom, they tend to dislike a single routine. This resource presents choices of activities to help students make connections between their lives and Shakespeare's *Macbeth.* The activities afford students opportunities to read, write, think, speak, and act out in response to the play.

In developing these activities, I've drawn upon research in effective teaching, reading, whole language, and English education as well as my experience as a classroom teacher. I have also had the opportunities to team teach with my friends and colleagues, Sue Ellen Savereide, instructor at the Malcolm Price Laboratory School, Cedar Falls, Iowa, and Sharon Palas, English teacher at Denver High School, Denver, Iowa, in developing these materials.

Although these activities will help get your students involved with *Macbeth,* I don't propose that these are the only ones that work with students. As the teacher, you determine which activities the students should use, and whether they should work individually, in pairs, small groups, or as an entire class. You also need to decide whether the students should read silently, aloud, or in combination. I also encourage you to continue using the films and professional recordings of the play that have worked in the past: both films and recordings may be used as prereading, reading, or postreading techniques. In addition to the ideas I present here, I urge you to develop your own specific improvisations, questions, and extending activities that reflect your specific teaching objectives and that best fit your district's curriculum.

John Wilson Swope

About the Author

In addition to eleven years as a middle and secondary English, speech, and drama teacher, John Wilson Swope has taught English education courses at the University of Florida and the University of Northern Iowa, where he is currently an assistant professor of English. His articles and reviews have appeared in *English Journal, English Leadership Quarterly, FOCUS, The Leaflet,* and *The Virginia English Bulletin.* He is a frequent presenter at conferences sponsored by the National Council of Teachers of English and its local affiliates. As an actor, director, and designer, he has participated in more than a dozen community theater productions.

Table of Contents

ACT II

ACT IV

Focusing Activities

Prereading Activities

During-reading Activities

Postreading Activities

ACT V

Focusing Activities

Prereading Activities

During-reading Activities

PART ONE

Suggestions to the Teacher

A Guide to Using This Resource

READING PROCESSES

In recent years, teachers have come to teach writing as a process of prewriting, writing, and rewriting. Approaching reading as a similar process of prereading, during-reading, and postreading allows students to assimilate difficult texts systematically, enhancing the students' comprehension, understanding, and appreciation. As a linguistic process, effective reading involves the reader: the reader anticipates what the text may reveal, reads to confirm or contradict those goals, and then thinks about what has been read.

To guide you in using reading as a process to teach *Macbeth,* this section will

- explain reading processes;

- establish a rationale for using a reading process approach to *Macbeth*;

- explain the overall organization of the student activities in this resource;

- explain the function of each of the various activities in this resource.

All activities follow a reading processes model and fall into the following three major groups, with a fourth group of optional activities called *extending activities*.

Prereading activities help students assess and organize information or personal experience that relates to what they will read. These activities help students to connect their prior knowledge to the text as well as help them establish a genuine purpose for reading it.

During-reading activities encourage students to read actively rather than passively, taking more responsibility for their own learning. Because full comprehension of a text doesn't occur immediately upon reading it the first time, students often need help to make sense of what they've just read. By structuring reading sessions and using reading, writing, speaking, listening, viewing, and critical thinking activities to foster active contemplation of the text, students can begin to explore their possible interpretations of the text.

Postreading activities help students make sense of their earlier explorations of the literature and come to an overall understanding of a work.

Extending activities allow students to apply what they've learned about the text to new situations after they've reached an understanding of the work.

RATIONALE

Reading *Macbeth* is difficult, even for the most proficient students. As teachers, when we read the play along with our classes, we may be reading the text for the tenth or twentieth time. We may forget that our students are encountering this text for the first time. As teachers and students of literature ourselves, we have developed our appreciation, understanding, interpretations, and love of Shakespeare's plays through our repeated exposure to them. We have read, reread, contemplated, researched, discussed, listened to, and viewed performances of them. The activities in this resource apply a reading process approach to the study of *Macbeth* and encourage students to read, reread, contemplate, discuss, listen to, and view the play as active readers and learners, enhancing their understanding, appreciation, and enjoyment of it.

This resource provides you with choices of activities to help students understand *Macbeth*. The selection of activities depends upon the students you teach, your instructional goals, and the time you wish to devote to the study of the play. For example, a brief unit on *Macbeth* using these materials would include

🙦 completing one focusing activity and reviewing the plot summary for a specific scene as prereading activity,

🙦 keeping either a character diary or a response journal throughout the reading of the play as a during-reading activity,

🙦 completing one of the postreading activities.

The *vocabulary, viewing a scene on videotape, guides to character development, critical thinking questions, language exploration,* and *extending activities* are other options to achieve additional instructional goals.

ORGANIZATION OF THE ACTIVITIES

To facilitate the planning of your unit, I've grouped the students' activities according to act. For each act, I've arranged the activities according to stage of the reading process: prereading, during-reading, or postreading. (*See* Figure 1: Summary of Reading Process Activities for *Macbeth* located at the end of Part One.) Extending activities, designed for use only after a complete reading of the play, follow the materials for Act V. Answer keys for quizzes and suggested answers for discussion activities are located in Appendix C.

PREREADING ACTIVITIES

The prereading activities for *Macbeth* include focusing activities, vocabulary, and plot summaries.

Focusing Activities

All focusing activities share a common goal: to help students organize and apply relevant prior knowledge and experience to the scene they are about to read. Because they set the stage for reading, they should be brief, generally between five and ten minutes. These activities help establish a genuine purpose for reading by encouraging students to speculate about what *may* happen rather than to predict accurately what *does happen* in the play. Although several different focusing activities are available for each scene of the play, students need to complete *only one* of them: scenarios for improvisation, prereading discussion questions, speculation journal, or introducing the play with videotape.

Scenarios for Improvisation. These improvisational group activities take a few minutes for students to prepare and present but allow them to explore the possible motives and actions of characters in situations that relate to a particular scene. Once they present an improvisation to the class, it becomes a common experience and a part of each person's relevant prior knowledge. A brief discussion of the improvisation will help connect the improvisation to the action of the play. After reading, the students may wish to discuss the similarities between the improvisation and what actually happened in the scene.

Prereading Discussion Questions. As an anticipatory device, these questions allow students to talk through their speculations about what they will read. The questions tend to be more effective once everyone has become familiar with the play and its characters.

Speculation Journal. This activity begins as an individual writing-to-learn activity. After students speculate for three to five minutes about what *might* happen, encourage them to share their predictions. Keep in mind that the goal is for them to use what they know about characters and motivations, to explore what logically *could* happen and not to guess correctly what *does* happen.

Introducing the Play with Videotape. Showing the opening scenes of a play before students begin reading it can be an excellent introductory focusing activity. A visual presentation provides them with a sense of the setting and overall action of the scene before they confront the written text. After showing the film or tape, ask the class, "What seems to be going on here?" A few minutes' discussion will help you determine if the class has a general sense of what they've seen.

Vocabulary

The vocabulary activities allow students to expand their vocabularies through repeated exposure to words within context. The words defined in the prereading lists are the bases for both the postreading vocabulary activities: *vocabulary in context* and *vocabulary review quiz*. Although most of the words on these lists are in common use today, Shakespeare often used the words in different contexts than contemporary speakers. The lists provide brief definitions and synonyms as well as a sentence to illustrate the word in a context similar to the one the students will encounter in the play.

Plot Summaries

Once the students have completed a focusing activity, share the plot summary of the scene with them before they begin reading it. Reading the summary helps students establish the overall direction for the scene before beginning Shakespeare's verse. With the summary as a road map, students are less likely to get lost among Shakespeare's many literary allusions.

DURING-READING ACTIVITIES

Students need to read actively. When the text is as challenging as *Macbeth,* few students can comprehend it immediately. Instead, most of them need to contemplate the text consciously to make sense of it. During-reading activities allow them to reread, write, talk, listen, view, and think about what they've just read.

Four types of activities enable students to contemplate actively what they've just read, to begin to explore possible interpretations of it: *response journal, character diary, viewing scenes on videotape,* and *guides to character development.*

Response Journal

This writing-to-learn activity is based upon the work of David Bleich. The students make four types of responses either while they read or immediately upon completing the reading of a particular scene. They respond emotionally to what they're reading and try to speculate why the text provokes a particular response. Then they record and explore their own associations and experiences that relate to the text. The figurative response then draws the students back to the text, making them contemplate an important section of it. Finally, the response journal encourages students to record the questions that arise while they read, so they can address them later.

All students keep an individual response journal throughout their reading of *Macbeth.* They use it as a means to record their reactions to what they read either while they read or immediately upon completing a reading session. For example, if students read the play aloud during class, encourage them to take the last few minutes of the period to write in their response journals. If the students are to read outside of class, then also have them complete their response journals as part of the homework assignment. This writing in the response journal is exploratory in nature: it is a forum for formulating and testing hypotheses about the play, its language, and its characters; it is not a place where grammar, usage, and mechanics are an issue.

Character Diary

An alternative to the response journal, this exploratory writing-to-learn activity encourages students to read actively and to contemplate what they've read. The students summarize the action of the play, in the form of a personal diary, from the perspective of a character. Because no character is present for all the action of a play, the character diary requires students to provide a logical account of how their individual character comes to know the action. This paraphrasing not only improves the students' reading comprehension but affects a broad range of related language skills, "including literal recall of events, characters, main points, rhetorical features, stylistic devices and text structure" (Brown and Cambourne, 9). Like the response journal, the writing in the character diary is exploratory in nature.

Viewing a Scene on Videotape

As an optional during-reading activity, students may view and discuss several scenes immediately after having read them. These include Macbeth and Banquo's first meeting with the witches (Act I, scene iii), Macbeth and Lady Macbeth's reactions to their murdering Duncan (Act II, scene ii), the appearance of Banquo's ghost at the banquet (Act III, scene iv), Macbeth's second meeting with the witches (Act IV, scene i), and Lady Macbeth's sleepwalking (Act V, scene i).

Note that if you use Orson Welles' production, the sequence of scenes is different from most play texts. Most notably, many early scenes have been omitted and Lady Macbeth's sleepwalking scene immediately precedes her suicide. The PBS/BBC production is a fuller treatment of the play. If you choose to use the Polanski production, preview it first for its violent and sexual content.

Because the students will already be familiar with the play's language, action, and characters, viewing the scene permits them to use the additional visual and auditory information to improve their understanding of the play's language and characters. For example, seeing professional actors portray Macbeth and Lady Macbeth as they react to their murdering of Duncan demonstrates his horror at the regicide in contrast to her sense of political expediency. Likewise, letting students see professional actors react to Macbeth's confrontation of Banquo's ghost may make more sense than their just reading it.

Guides to Character Development

These guides are additional, optional means to structure the students' contemplation of a play. Seven sets of guides to character development and revelation include Macbeth, Lady Macbeth, and Banquo, or Macduff, as major characters and Malcolm, Ross, and the witches as minor ones.

How you use these activities depends on the specific goals for studying *Macbeth*. For example, you can have the entire class examine how Shakespeare develops a major character by having them choose to examine Macbeth, Lady Macbeth, Banquo, or Macduff. Similarly, they may examine how Shakespeare reveals minor and more static characters like Malcolm or Ross. Have them complete these activities individually, in pairs, or in small groups.

These charts direct students first to review specific portions of the play to determine what characters do, say, or what other characters say about them before drawing conclusions about what insight this information provides into a specific character. You will find charts for the characters with the during-reading materials for each act in which the specific character appears. In terms of major characters, only Macbeth appears in all five acts, but Lady Macbeth appears in all but Act IV. Banquo is present in the first three acts, while Macduff appears in Acts II, IV, and V. As minor characters, Malcolm appears in all but Act III, the witches in Acts I, III, and IV, and Ross in all five.

POSTREADING ACTIVITIES

Postreading activities help students read, write, talk, or act their ways through the play to reach an overall understanding of it. This resource provides four types of postreading activities: *comprehension checks, critical thinking questions, language exploration,* and *vocabulary.*

Comprehension Checks

Two types of activities assess the students' comprehension of the text that they've read: a *multiple choice quiz* and *small group discussion questions.*

Comprehension Check (multiple choice). The quizzes consist of five multiple choice questions for each act. Two are factual, two are interpretative, and one is evaluative.

Small Group Discussion Questions to Check Comprehension. These questions help students assess whether they understand key issues of a play. Encourage them to discuss their answers with one another and return to the text to clarify misunderstandings through collaborative discussion in small groups.

Critical Thinking Questions

Postreading discussion questions are probably the most common device used in literature classrooms. However, questions need to do more than simply check whether or not the students have read a particular passage. The Critical Thinking Questions follow the model of Christenbury and Kelly, and help students connect the act that they've just read with the play as a whole, to their personal experiences, and to other literary experiences. To establish the goal for the discussion, present the focus question first. Although this question is the one that students will find difficult to answer at first, present it to them and just let them think about it. Explore the related issues in the other questions and then have the students return to the focus question to connect their other responses to it.

Language Exploration

These activities allow students to return to the text and explore how Shakespeare uses language within the context of the acts of the play that they've already read. Encourage them to use these activities to review and apply concepts and to develop interpretations of specific passages. The concepts in *Macbeth* include *figurative language* (simile and metaphor, personification, and apostrophe), *symbol, sensory imagery,* and *irony.*

Vocabulary Activities

Vocabulary in Context. For a postreading activity, students can examine how Shakespeare uses the prereading vocabulary within a specific passage. Then the students can apply an appropriate meaning and develop an interpretation of the passage within the context of the play. Although these activities direct students to excerpts, you can encourage students to review an entire section of a particular scene to establish a more complete context.

Vocabulary Review Quizzes. These activities provide students with ways to assess their mastery of vocabulary for each act. The quiz items deliberately repeat, in modern language, the context established in the vocabulary in context activities. These quizzes are in a multiple choice format to facilitate evaluation.

EXTENDING ACTIVITIES

Extending activities encourage students to apply what they've learned from studying *Macbeth* to alternative situations. They may complete these activities individually or in groups. This resource includes general directions for extending activities as well as more specific directions for acting out, oral interpretation, using puppet theater, making masks, and writing assignments.

Acting Out

Through improvisations, students can work out a skit to portray a particular scene or place a familiar character in a different context.

Oral Interpretation

These activities encourage students to present scenes from the play in its original language. With the suggested scenes, students can work either individually or in pairs. The directions include steps for preparing an effective oral interpretation. Students may want to incorporate either puppet theater or masks into their presentations.

Puppet Theater

This activity includes directions for making paper bag puppets and suggestions for two, three, or more performers for specific scenes.

Paper Plate Masks

Masks provide a way to present visual interpretations of a character. Students can do this easily by constructing simple masks from paper plates as shown. These masks, like the puppets, may also be combined with oral or dramatic presentations.

Writing Assignments

Writing tasks give students a chance to incorporate their new understanding of the play into a piece of writing. To develop these assignments, they may want to use some of their reading process activities, such as response journals or character diaries, as sources for prewriting.

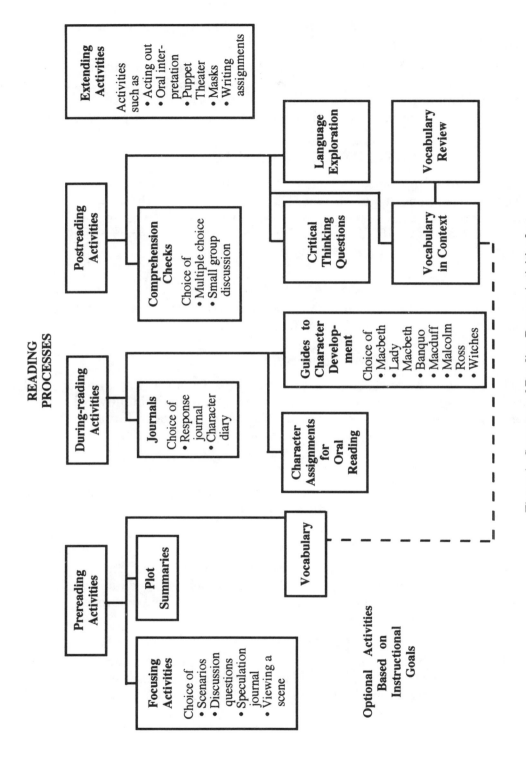

READING PROCESSES

Prereading Activities

Focusing Activities

Choice of
• Scenarios
• Discussion questions
• Speculation journal
• Viewing a scene

Plot Summaries

Vocabulary

During-reading Activities

Journals

Choice of
• Response journal
• Character diary

Character Assignments for Oral Reading

Guides to Character Development

Choice of
• Macbeth
• Lady Macbeth
• Banquo
• Macduff
• Malcolm
• Ross
• Witches

Postreading Activities

Comprehension Checks

Choice of
• Multiple choice
• Small group discussion

Critical Thinking Questions

Language Exploration

Vocabulary in Context

Vocabulary Review

Extending Activities

Activities such as
• Acting out
• Oral interpretation
• Puppet Theater
• Masks
• Writing assignments

Optional Activities Based on Instructional Goals

Figure 1: Summary of Reading Process Activities for <u>Macbeth</u>

10

PART TWO

Ready-to-Use Materials for the Student

INTRODUCTORY MATERIALS
FOR
TEACHING SHAKESPEARE

William Shakespeare

William Shakespeare
April 23, 1564–April 23, 1616

William Shakespeare was the eldest son and third child of John Shakespeare and Mary Arden. His father was a maker of white leather (whittawer) and gloves (glover), and a wool dealer as well as a yeoman farmer who owned his own land. As a prosperous and respected tradesman, John Shakespeare also took part in the local government of Stratford and held several government positions including Chamberlain (town treasurer), Alderman (town councilman), and Bailiff of Stratford-upon-Avon.

During William's childhood, Stratford was a prosperous, self-governing market town. As a result, the Corporation of Stratford maintained the grammar school originally founded by the medieval Gild of the Holy Cross where historians believe young William received his early education. The school's gildhall was also where traveling companies of actors probably performed. Records of the town suggest that William may have seen his first plays during his boyhood. The Chamberlain's accounts show that different companies of traveling players appeared and were paid from the borough's accounts on more than thirty occasions.

Town and church documents also show that William Shakespeare married Ann Hathaway when he was eighteen and she was twenty-six in 1582. They had three children, Susanna (1583) and twins Hamnet (1585–96) and Judith (1585–1662).

Shortly after his children were born, Shakespeare left Stratford and nothing is known of his life until he began acting in London in 1592. In London, he acted and served as a reviser and writer of plays. At age twenty-eight, he began to impress his contemporaries with the quality and popularity of his work. He published his first narrative poem, *Venus and Adonis* in 1593 and *The Rape of Lucrece* the following year.

While living in London, Shakespeare acted with several companies including the Chamberlain's Men (later called the King's Men) who provided entertainment for the Royal Court. He wrote many of his plays for his own acting company. Shakespeare was also partner in several theatrical ventures including being one of the proprietors of the Globe theater that was built just outside the city limits of London in 1599. His partners in the Globe also included famous actors of the day—Richard Burbage, Will Kempe, John Heminge, and Henry Condell. Heminge and Condell would publish the first collected editions of Shakespeare's plays, known as the First Folio, in 1623.

Although Shakespeare continued to live and work in London until 1610, he purchased New Place, one of the largest houses in Stratford in 1597. When he retired to New Place in 1610, he was a wealthy landowner whose estate included farmland, pasture, and gardens. Making occasional visits to London until 1614, Shakespeare continued to associate with actors and playwrights for the rest of his life. While in retirement at Stratford, he surrounded himself with family and friends. Shakespeare died at home on April 23, St. George's Day in 1616. He was buried in the chancel of Holy Trinity Church in Stratford. He willed New Place to his elder daughter Susanna, then wife of Dr. John Hall. The poet's widow probably lived there with the Halls until her death in 1623. Within a few years of Shakespeare's death, a monument to him was erected and placed on the north wall of Westminster Abbey in London.

© 1994 by The Center for Applied Research in Education

An Introduction to Shakespeare's Language

Because Shakespeare wrote nearly four hundred years ago, some of the conventions that he uses in his plays present problems for modern readers. Most of Shakespeare's lines are written in poetry. Although these lines don't usually rhyme, they do have a set rhythm (called *meter*). To achieve the meter, Shakespeare arranges words so that the syllables which are stressed or said more loudly than others fall in a regular pattern: dah DUM dah DUM dah DUM dah DUM dah DUM. For example, read the following lines from *Macbeth* aloud:

ᴥ

True worthy Banquo—he is full so valiant
And in his commendation I am fed.

ᴥ

Because you are familiar with the words that Shakespeare uses here, you naturally stressed every second syllable:

ᴥ

true WORthy BANquo—HE is FULL so VALiant
and IN his COMmenDAtion I am FED.

ᴥ

The pattern of one unstressed syllable followed by a stressed one, dah DUM, is called an *iamb*. Each pattern is referred to as a *foot*. Because Shakespeare uses five iambic feet to a line, this pattern in known as *iambic pentameter*.

In order for Shakespeare to maintain the set meter of most lines, he often structures the lines differently than normal English speech. He may change the normal order of words so that the stressed syllables fall in the appropriate place. For example, the following sentence has no set meter:

ᴥ

I'll FIGHT 'til my FLESH be HACKED from my BONES.

ᴥ

However, Shakespeare turns these words around a bit to maintain the meter in *Macbeth*:

❧

I'll FIGHT till FROM my BONES my FLESH be HACKED.

❧

He may shorten words by omitting letters so that a two-syllable word is one syllable. As a result, *over* often appears as *o'er* and *'tis* in place of *it is*.

Shakespeare also uses forms of words that we rarely use today, four hundred years later. Among these are the personal pronouns *thou* (you), *thine* (your, yours), *thee* (you as in "to you"), and *thyself* (yourself). Often Shakespeare also uses verb endings that we no longer use. For example, *hath* is an old form of *has*, and *art* an older form of *are*. You're also likely to encounter several words or phrases that we no longer use at all: *anon* instead of *soon* or *shortly*, or *prithee* meaning *I pray to thee (you)*.

Conventions of Shakespeare's Staging

When we attend theatrical performances—school plays, assembly programs, or movies in public theaters—we're accustomed to finding a seat and waiting until the lights dim, the audience quiets down, and the play or feature begins. We're also used to seeing scenery that suggests the location of the play and expect the stage lighting to help set the mood.

But all this was not so in Shakespeare's time. Then people attended plays during the day, for there was no way to light the stage effectively once the sun had set. Public performance of plays in theaters was a fairly new idea at the time because the first permanent English theater had been built less than twenty years before Shakespeare began writing his plays. Although the shape of the theaters varied from square, circular, or octagon, all had a stage that was simply a raised platform in an open yard surrounded with tiers of galleries to accommodate the spectators. The stage was covered with a roof, commonly called "The Heavens." While the roof protected the actors from the weather, the attic space above could hold machinery, such as ropes and pulleys to lower thrones or heavenly deities to the stage or to hide the sound effects of thunder, alarum bells, or cannonades. By modern standards these theaters were small. The open yard in front of the stage in one theater measured only fifty-five feet across. Up to two thousand spectators could either sit on benches in the tiers of galleries or stand in the open yard in front of the stage.

These theaters used simple stage props—chairs or tables were brought on the raised platform as needed. Actual scenery may have been suggested through dialogue or may have included minimal set pieces such as a few trees to suggest a forest, or a rock to suggest a river bank. The stages themselves had many built-in acting areas that could function in a number of ways: for instance, small inner stages with drapes which the actors used as inner rooms or raised balconies. The actors could use the inner room for King Duncan's chamber in *Macbeth* or Brutus' tent in *Julius Caesar*. The balcony might serve as Juliet's balcony in *Romeo and Juliet* or as the battlements of Elsinore Castle in *Hamlet.*

The costumes were based on the contemporary clothing styles of the time. Instead of attempting any sort of accurate historical costuming, the actors wore clothes that were as much like those of a character's rank. For example, Macbeth would have been costumed as any nobleman and Lady Capulet as any wealthy English merchant's wife. Occasionally, other costume pieces may have been added to suggest witches, fairies, national or racial costumes.

During the time that Shakespeare wrote and acted, only three or four professional companies performed in theaters just outside the limits of London. These professional troupes employed male actors only. Although most of the roles in Shakespeare's plays are male, the few parts of younger female characters—Juliet or her mother in *Romeo and Juliet*, for instance—were played by young boys, aged fourteen or so and apprenticed to actors. Men may have played some female roles, especially those of older, comedic women, such as Juliet's Nurse.

Principal Locations for *Macbeth*

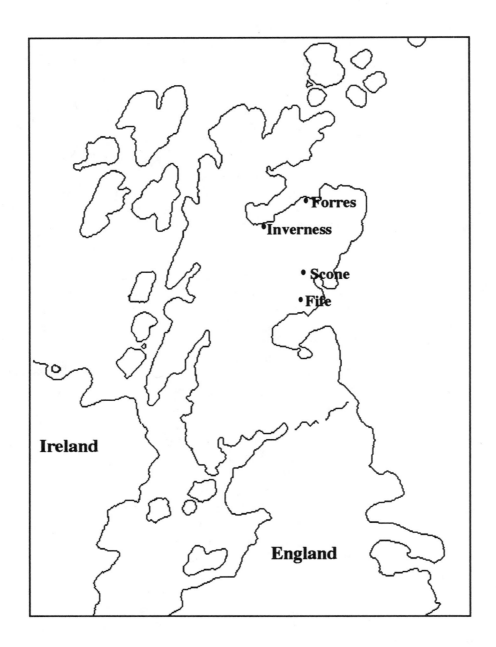

ACT I

NAME:_____   DATE:_____

Focusing Activities
for
Macbeth
Scenarios for Improvisation
Act I

Directions: Presented below are locations and situations involving characters. As your teacher directs you, and before reading an individual scene, pretend to be one of the characters and act out the situation. Don't worry about speaking like the characters in Shakespeare's plays, just try to imagine how you would react to each situation and use your own language. Your teacher may give you a few minutes to discuss what you would like to do with the other performers. Your teacher will probably ask you to act out your scene for others in the class. When you finish, your teacher may ask your classmates to discuss what they've seen.

scene iii. *Scene*: A carnival.

Characters: Mac, Ben, and a gypsy fortuneteller.

Situation: Mac and Ben are spending the evening at a local carnival. On a dare from Ben, Mac decides to go into the gypsy's tent and have his palm read. The fortuneteller informs Mac that he will soon receive news that will change his life and bring him great fame. Ben comes in and tells Mac that he's won a full scholarship to Harvard. How does Mac respond?

scene v. *Scene*: Macbeth's castle.

Character: *Lady Macbeth*

Situation: Lady Macbeth has just received a letter from her husband informing her of his meeting with the witches, the prophecies, and his new title. How does she respond to the news?

scene vi. *Scene*: Macbeth's castle.

Characters: Lady Macbeth and King Duncan.

Situation: The King has just arrived. Give Lady Macbeth's welcoming speech and the king's reply.

scene vii. *Scene*: Macbeth's castle during the banquet.

Characters: Macbeth and Lady Macbeth.

Situation: Macbeth begins to have doubts about murdering Duncan. Lady Macbeth convinces him to do it. Improvise the scene between them.

23

Focusing Activities
for
Macbeth
Small Group Discussion Questions
Act I

Directions: Before reading scenes in Act I, discuss the following questions in small groups. You may want to make notes about your discussion so you can share them with classmates or refer back to them after you've read the scene.

scenes i and ii.

1. Based upon what you may have heard or seen, what do you think happens in the play, *Macbeth*?

2. Why do you think the witches appear before other characters?

scene ii.   If you were a king or queen with absolute power, how would you punish one of your nobles who had tried to overthrow you? How would you reward one who helped you put down a rebellion?

scene iii.   What do you think the witches will tell Macbeth, and how do you expect him to react?

scene iv. If you were Macbeth, how would you respond to learning that the King had decided to make his son the official heir to the throne?

scene v. If you were Lady Macbeth, how would you react to the news of Macbeth's encounter with the witches and his new title?

scene vi. Based upon what you've already seen of Lady Macbeth, how do you expect her to greet the King?

scene vii. Why might Macbeth begin to doubt whether he can commit the murder?

NAME: _____   DATE:_____

Focusing Activities for *Macbeth*
Speculation Journal
Act I

Directions: This activity is to help you become involved actively with reading the play by helping you to determine a definite purpose for reading. Before you read these scenes in Act I, take a few minutes to respond in writing to the questions below. Don't worry about correct answers here. Use your own experience, what you know, or what you may have heard about the play to speculate about what you think might happen. Sometimes, as for scenes i, ii, and iv below, you may be asked to speculate about issues that parallel the action of the play. After reading a scene, you may find that the characters reacted differently than you thought. Don't worry about these differences; just make note of them because you will have opportunities to share these differences in other activities.

scene i. Based upon what you have seen or heard, what do you expect *Macbeth* to be about?

scene ii. If you were a king or queen with absolute power, how would you punish one of your nobles who had tried to overthrow you? How would you reward one who helped you put down a rebellion?

scene iii. What might the witches tell Macbeth, and how might he react?

scene iv. If you were Macbeth, how would you respond to learning that the King had decided to make his son the official heir to the throne?

scene v. How do you think Lady Macbeth will react to her husband's news of his encounter with the witches and his new title?

scene vi. If you were Lady Macbeth, how would you greet the king?

scene vii. If Macbeth were to begin doubting his ability to follow through with the murder, how do you think his wife would react?

After reading Act I: Now that you have finished reading Act I, which of your speculations were most accurate? How do you account for them? Which ones were least like the action of the play? Why do you think you speculated as you did?

**Focusing Activity
for
Macbeth
*Introducing the Play with Videotape***

Directions: Before you begin reading *Macbeth*, you will view a video version of the opening scenes. Don't worry about trying to understand everything, just go for general impressions. As you watch, you may want to note any questions you need to ask your teacher afterwards. After viewing the scene, take a few minutes to respond to the questions below.

1. In your own words, describe what you saw briefly. What seems to be the overall conflict or problem?

2. Where does each of the scenes take place? Which particular details help you to understand the action?

3. What kinds of things can the director of the film or video version do in this scene that could not be done in a live production of the play on stage?

NAME:_____   DATE:_____

Prereading Activity
for
Macbeth
Vocabulary
Act I

Directions: Shakespeare uses the following words in Act I. The section below provides a brief definition of each word and provides a sentence to illustrate its meaning. You may want to review the words for a particular scene before reading it.

Definitions

scene ii.

1. **plight:**   (n.). unfavorable state, situation, or condition.
   Example: From the man's *plight*, we concluded that he was probably homeless.

2. **broil:**   (n.) quarrel, brawl, or battle.
   Example: Once the fight broke out in center field, the baseball fans were eager to join the *broil*.

3. **disdain:**   (v.) to treat or look upon with contempt; unworthy of notice.
   Example: Once Jeff sold his idea for the video game to a major manufacturer, he *disdained* anyone who laughed at his original idea.

4. **vantage:**   (n.) advantage, benefit, or gain.
   Example: Once the competitor stopped selling gasoline, the convenience store saw *vantage* in raising its prices a nickel per gallon.

5. **flout:**   (n.) to treat with disdain, scorn, or contempt.
   Example: After our team won the championship, it was hard for us not to *flout* our victory to our opponents.

scene iii.

6. **intelligence**: (n.) knowledge of an event; information.
   Example: Because the school mailed report cards to parents directly, our neighbors had *intelligence* that their son might not graduate with his class.

7. **corporal:** (adj.) belonging to the material world.
   Example: Before the witches disappeared, they seemed to be *corporal* beings: poor, ragged, old women.

scene iv.

8. **harbinger**: (n.) herald; messenger; a person sent in advance of a royal train or troops to secure lodging.
   Example: Acting as *harbinger*, the chair of the local political party secured lodging for the candidate in private homes.

scene v.

9. **weird:** (adj.) concerning or controlling fate or destiny; unearthly.
   Example: It was *weird* that Jamie received a check from a distant relative on the same day that her horoscope had said she'd receive good news from an unknown source.

10. **impede:** (v.) to hinder, obstruct.
    Example: As a last attempt to *impede* the start of the new highway, the protesters lay down in front of the construction equipment.

Prereading Activity
for
Macbeth
Plot Summaries
Act I

Directions: To help you better understand and follow *Macbeth*, read the summary of a specific scene before you begin to read it. If you get lost during the scene, you can refer to the summary.

Act I,
scene i
In some unspecified place, in the middle of fog and filthy air, the witches plan to meet with Macbeth after the battle.

Act I,
scene ii
King Duncan's armies have recently battled the armies of Macdonwald near Forres. King Duncan, his sons, Malcolm and Donalbain, and Lennox encounter a wounded Captain and inquire about the course of the battle. The captain informs them that just when the battle seemed lost to Macdonwald's rebel forces, Macbeth rallied the forces, killed Macdonwald, an ally of the Swedo, King of Norway, and placed the rebel's head upon a pike on the battlements of the castle. As soon as it seemed that Macbeth had rallied the forces and won the battle, the Norwegian forces attacked. The Captain was wounded and could not tell how the battle went from then on. The attendants take the Captain to the surgeon for attention.

Ross, another of the Scottish noblemen loyal to Duncan, enters. He informs King Duncan that the Norwegians attacked along with the support of the Scottish Thane of Cawdor. However, King Duncan's armies prevailed. The Scottish armies refused to allow the Norwegians to bury their dead until King Swedo agreed to pay $10,000.

Because the Thane of Cawdor has betrayed King Duncan, the king strips him of his title and lands and decides to award the title of Thane of Cawdor to Macbeth for his bravery.

Act I,
scene iii
Somewhere upon the heath during a foul storm, the three witches reappear. The first witch has decided to take revenge upon a sailor's wife who wouldn't share chestnuts. She proposes to sail a sieve to his ship, *Tiger*, and board it in the form of a tailless rat, so that she can cause problems for the sailor.

Macbeth and Banquo, another general loyal to King Duncan, enter. Macbeth comments upon the foulness of the weather and then notices the witches. Macbeth describes them as women with beards and doesn't

31

know whether they're real or some sort of demons. He demands that they speak.

They address him by name and title. First as Macbeth, Thane of Glamis, then as Macbeth, Thane of Cawdor, and finally as Macbeth, future King of Scotland.

Macbeth is amazed at these prophecies: he knows he is Thane of Glamis, but doesn't yet know that King Duncan has made him Thane of Cawdor. When Banquo addresses the witches, they turn and tell him that he is both lesser than Macbeth and greater, for he won't be King of Scotland but his children shall be.

Macbeth demands to know how the witches' prophecies can be true, but they vanish without explaining. Ross and Angus enter and inform Macbeth that King Duncan has named him Thane of Cawdor. Macbeth and Banquo comment to themselves that the first part of the witches' prophecies has come true and wonder how the rest will come to pass.

To himself, Macbeth admits that while he's pleased with his good fortune, he's uneasy about the rest of the witches' prophecies. Macbeth and Banquo go to meet the king.

Act I, scene iv

In the Duncans' palace at Forres, Malcolm reports to his father that the former Thane of Cawdor has been executed for treason. When Macbeth enters with Banquo, he thanks the king for his new title and reaffirms his loyalty to Duncan.

Duncan responds and again thanks Macbeth and Banquo. Duncan then formally names his eldest son, Malcolm, Prince of Cumberland and heir to the throne. Duncan announces that the court will go to Inverness, Macbeth's castle.

Macbeth realizes that if he is to become king, he will have to overcome Malcolm. He recognizes that his desire to be king may lead him to evil. Macbeth leaves for Inverness, so that he will arrive ahead of the king.

Act I, scene v

At Inverness, Lady Macbeth reads aloud from her husband's letter. He tells her of his encounter with the witches and their prophecies that have come true. To herself, Lady Macbeth vows to help Macbeth become all that the witches promised. She also comments that her husband is often too compassionate and lacking in ambition, but she will help him.

An attendant comes and informs Lady Macbeth that the king is coming to Inverness tonight. Lady Macbeth realizes that this is the opportunity she and Macbeth need to murder Duncan. Macbeth enters and confirms that the king will stay the night at Inverness before going on to the formal investiture of Malcolm. Lady Macbeth promises that Duncan will not see the rising sun. She tells Macbeth not to let his face betray their plans to murder Duncan.

Act I, scene vi   When the royal court arrives, Lady Macbeth greets the members as the perfect hostess, escorting the king into the castle.

Act I, scene vii   Later that evening, Macbeth slips away from the banquet and contemplates the plan to murder the king. He wishes that the murder were over and done with. He fears being caught. Macbeth feels that he will betray Duncan in two ways; first, because he is the king's first cousin, and second, because murdering the king will disrupt the order of the world—kings are God's chosen representatives.

Lady Macbeth enters and chides her husband for acting suspiciously and leaving the banquet, because the king keeps asking for him. When Macbeth tries to call off the plot, Lady Macbeth won't hear of it. When Macbeth suggests that they may fail, Lady Macbeth reveals that Duncan will sleep soundly because he's tired. Then she'll make sure the king's guards are drunk enough so that they'll sleep soundly. She will make sure the guards end up with the murder weapons, the bloody daggers—so they will then be immediately killed as the murderers.

Class Period:

CHARACTER ASSIGNMENTS FOR ORAL READING GROUPS
Macbeth

Session 1: Act I, scenes i, ii, iii

Characters	Group 1	Group 2	Group 3	Group 4
First Witch	_____	_____	_____	_____
Second Witch	_____	_____	_____	_____
Third Witch	_____	_____	_____	_____
Duncan	_____	_____	_____	_____
Captain, Banquo	_____	_____	_____	_____
Malcolm, Angus	_____	_____	_____	_____
Ross	_____	_____	_____	_____
Macbeth	_____	_____	_____	_____

34

Class Period:

CHARACTER ASSIGNMENTS FOR ORAL READING GROUPS
Macbeth

Session 2: Act I, scenes iv, v, vi, vii

Characters	*Group 1*	*Group 2*	*Group 3*	*Group 4*
Macbeth (scene iv, v)	___	___	___	___
Macbeth (scene vii)	___	___	___	___
Lady Macbeth (scene iv, v)	___	___	___	___
Lady Macbeth (scene vii)	___	___	___	___
Attendant	___	___	___	___
Duncan	___	___	___	___
Banquo	___	___	___	___
Malcolm	___	___	___	___

35

During-reading Activity
for
Macbeth
Directions for Response Journal

Although we often read silently, reading is an active process. As we run our eyes across a line of text, we transform the letters and words into mental images. The words have the power to affect us in many ways. The purpose of this response journal is to help you as a reader verbalize several different types of responses immediately after you've read, and to assist you in recalling the experiences of reading prior to discussion with your classmates.

Your response journal is a place for you to react to what you read personally. This is also a place to begin piecing together your understanding of the play. Your journal is a place to think aloud on paper and not to have to worry about grammatical correctness or punctuation. You may prefer to do it as you read or immediately upon finishing a reading session. It won't be nearly as effective if you put it off! There are four types of responses you should make each time. None of these needs to be more than a brief paragraph, four paragraphs total.

1. *Respond emotionally.* How does the play make you feel at this point? Record your feelings in a few sentences and then explore them for a few minutes, trying to figure out why you feel as you do.

2. *Make associations between ideas in the text and your personal experience.* In what situations have you felt similar to the characters ? What persons, places, and ideas from your own experiences came to your mind while you were reading this portion of the play? Try to list three to five associations, but don't worry about trying to figure out why they came to mind. Just accept that they occur.

3. *Look at the language.* What portions of Shakespeare's language attracts your attention? These might be individual words, phrases, lines, scenes, or images. Make note of whatever feature(s) draw your attention. Speculate for a few minutes about what you think these might mean.

4. Record any questions or problems. Make note of any portion of the play, its language, or events that seem to cause you problems. Write down any questions that occur to you as you read.

Here's a sample journal for Act I, scene iii:

1. Macbeth and Banquo seem more intrigued by the witches than afraid of them. While the witches don't actually seem to work any magic, their reference to the sailor's wife suggests that they enjoy making trouble for mortals and seem to be evil. These witches seem to be true to the stereotype: ugly old women who cackle and brew cauldrons full of vile potions.

2. This scene reminds me of some stereotypical opening shot from a horror movie—lightning, storm coming around a spooky castle. I wonder how a director would stage it so the audience might not laugh.
Reminds me of the sequence in Walt Disney's "Snow White" when the queen makes the poisoned apple.
These three also remind me of the Witch of the West in "The Wizard of Oz." The witches' brew is as gross as the banquet in "Indiana Jones and the Temple of Doom."

3. Macbeth's line, "so foul and fair a day I have not seen," seems to suggest that the witches bring foul smells with them, like brimstone maybe.

4. Macbeth notices that these witches have beards like men, but seem to be women. Something seems to have been lost in the images of witches since Shakespeare's day. Why would having beards make the witches seem stranger?

During-reading Activity
for
Macbeth
Response Journal

Directions: Use the spaces below to record your responses to the act and scenes of *Macbeth* that you've just finished reading. Respond to all four sections and take a few additional minutes to explore why you responded as you did.

Response Journal for Act ____, scene ____ to Act ____, scene ____.

1. How does the play make you feel at this point? Record your emotional response(s) in a few sentences and then explore for a few minutes, trying to figure out why you feel as you do.

2. In what situations have you felt similar to the characters? What persons, places, and ideas from your own experiences came to your mind while you were reading this portion of the play? Try to list at least three associations, but don't worry about trying to figure out why they came to mind. Just accept that they occur.

   a.

   b.

   c.

3. What portions of Shakespeare's language attracts your attention? These might be individual words, phrases, lines, scenes, or images. Make note of whatever features draw your attention. Speculate for a few minutes about what you think they might mean.

4. Make note of any portion of the play, its language, or events that cause you problems. Note any questions that you might ask.

During-reading Activity
for
Macbeth
Directions for Character Diary

As you read *Macbeth*, you will find that the events of the play affect the lives of many characters, not just Macbeth. To give you an opportunity to explore the reactions of other characters, pretend to be one of the characters listed below. For this assignment, you will keep the personal diary of a single character for the time during which the play takes place.

Select one of the following characters for your diary:

Macbeth	Malcolm
Lady Macbeth	Fleance
Ross	Gentlewoman
Lennox	Seton
Porter (*see* Act II, scene iii)	Siward

In your diary, summarize the events of the act and provide an explanation for how your character may have heard of them, if the character was not involved with the events directly, and react as your character would. For example, Ross seems to be a minor character who first appears in Act I, scene ii. He is the one who first brings Macbeth the news that Duncan has named Macbeth Thane of Cawdor. Although he is not present in all the scenes, he is present as a member of the royal court and would have access to the rumors that might circulate there. Here is a sample of what his diary might look like after reading Act I, scene iii:

Macbeth didn't seem quite as surprised about King Duncan naming him Thane of Cawdor as I thought he'd be. It almost seems as though he was expecting it. Well there's much work to be done now that the rebellion is put down. The King awaits at Forres.

Acts and scenes	*Time and Place*
Act I, scene i	On a heath somewhere in Scotland
Act I, scene ii	On the edge of a battlefield near the king's palace at Forres
Act I, scene iii	On an isolated part of the heath
Act I, scene iv	A while later at the Royal palace at Forres
Act I, scene v	A day or so after Macbeth's encounter with the witches
Act I, scene vi	That evening, at the gate to Macbeth's castle

© 1994 by The Center for Applied Research in Education

Act I, scene vii	Later that evening, near the Great Hall of Macbeth's castle, Inverness
Act II, scene i	Outside Duncan's chambers in Macbeth's castle, in the early morning
Act II, scene ii	Outside Duncan's chambers, a short while later
Act II, scene iii	Gate to Macbeth's castle, immediately following
Act II, scene iv	Outside Macbeth's castle, next day
Act III, scene i	The Royal Palace at Forres, sometime after Macbeth's coronation
Act III, scene ii	The Queen's chambers, immediately following
Act III, scene iii	Before the Palace gate, that evening
Act III, scene iv	The Great Hall of the Palace, immediately following
Act III, scene v	On a heath, the same evening
Act III, scene vi	The Palace at Forres, the same evening
Act IV, scene i	A cavern, the next morning
Act IV, scene ii	Fife, Macduff's castle, a short while later
Act IV, scene iii	England, the king's palace, a week or so later
Act V, scene i	Macbeth's castle at Dunsinane, months later
Act V, scene ii	The country near Dunsinane, a short while later
Act V, scene iii	Inside the castle at Dunsinane, a short while later
Act V, scene iv	The country near Birnam Wood, a while later
Act V, scene v	Inside the castle, a while later
Act V, scene vi	Outside the castle, almost immediately
Act V, scene vii	Inside the castle, a short while later
Act V, scene viii	Inside the castle, a short while later
Act V, scene ix	In the Great Hall of the castle, after the battle

NAME:_____   DATE:_____

During-reading Activity
for
Macbeth
Character Diary 1
Act I, scenes i, ii, iii

Directions: Use the space below to record your character's reactions to the events of the first three scenes in Act I of *Macbeth*. Remember to include a summary of events, explain how your character learned of them, and give your character's reactions to them. Because this act has seven scenes, you may wish to record your character's entries as you read each scene. If you need additional room, use the back of this sheet.

The Personal Diary of

_____

(character's name)

Scotland

After the battle

_____

_____

_____

_____

_____

Later (scene ii)

_____

_____

_____

_____

_____

NAME:_____   DATE:_____

During-reading Activity
for
Macbeth
Character Diary 2
Act I, scenes iv, v, vi, vii

Directions: Use the space below to record your character's reactions to the events of the last four scenes in Act I of *Macbeth*. Remember to include a summary of events, explain how your character learned of them, and give your character's reactions to them. Because this act has seven scenes, you may want to record your character's entries as you read each scene. If you need additional room, use the back of this sheet.

The Personal Diary of

_____
(character's name)

Scene iv

Forres

_____
_____
_____
_____
_____
_____

Scenes v, vi, vii

Inverness, Macbeth's castle

_____
_____
_____
_____
_____
_____

During-reading Activity
for
Macbeth
Viewing Act I, scene iii
Macbeth and Banquo Meet the Three Witches

Directions: After you've read this scene, viewing a film or video version may help you better understand how the text translates into the characters' actions. Although you may want to keep your copy of the play handy, don't be surprised if the actors' script varies from yours. Film scripts often delete or reorder the lines in the play. You many want to note questions you need to ask your teacher afterwards. After viewing the scene, take a few minutes to respond to the questions below.

1. What do the costumes and the set representing a barren heath tell you about the time and place of the play?

2. What are Macbeth's and Banquo's attitudes towards the three witches?

3. How does Macbeth respond first to the witches' prophecies and then to the news that Angus and Ross bring him from King Duncan?

4. How do the actors' facial expressions, tones of voice, and gestures enhance Shakespeare's lines?

© 1994 by The Center for Applied Research in Education

During-reading Activity
for
Macbeth
Guide to Character Development: Macbeth
Act I

Shakespeare reveals his characters in four ways:

- through what the characters say to other characters in dialogue;
- through what the characters reveal about their thoughts through long speeches to the audience called *soliloquies*;
- through what other characters say about them;
- through what they do, their actions.

As you read the play, examine the following scenes for what they reveal about Macbeth's character and fill in the chart briefly using your own words. If you need more room, use the back of the page.

Scene	What Macbeth says, does or what others say about him	What this reveals about Macbeth's character
Act I, scene ii The Captain's description of Macbeth during the battle and Duncan's response		
Act I, scene iii Macbeth and Banquo meet the three witches		
Act I, scene iii Ross and Angus tell Macbeth about his new title		
Act I, scene iv Macbeth's response to Duncan about his new title		

Act I, scene iv Duncan names Malcolm Prince of Cumberland		
Act I, scene v Macbeth sends a letter to Lady Macbeth		
Act I, scene v Macbeth and Lady Macbeth plan for Duncan's visit		
Act I, scene vi Duncan arrives at Macbeth's castle		
Act I, scene vii Macbeth leaves the banquet for Duncan		

© 1994 by The Center for Applied Research in Education

NAME:_____   DATE:_____

During-reading Activity
for
Macbeth
Guide to Character Development: Lady Macbeth
Act I

Shakespeare reveals his characters in four ways:

- through what the characters say to other characters in dialogue;
- through what the characters reveal about their thoughts through long speeches to the audience called *soliloquies*;
- through what other characters say about them;
- through what they do, their actions.

As you read the play, examine the following scenes for what they reveal about Lady Macbeth's character and fill in the chart briefly using your own words. If you need more room, use the back of the page.

Scene	*What Lady Macbeth says, does or what others say about her*	*What this reveals about Lady Macbeth's character*
Act I, scene v Macbeth sends a letter to Lady Macbeth		
Act I, scene v Macbeth and Lady Macbeth plan for Duncan's visit		
Act I, scene vi Duncan arrives at Macbeth's castle		
Act I, scene vii Macbeth leaves the banquet for Duncan		

47

During-reading Activity
for
Macbeth
Guide to Character Development: Banquo
Act I

Shakespeare reveals his characters in four ways:

- through what the characters say to other characters in dialogue;
- through what the characters reveal about their thoughts through long speeches to the audience called *soliloquies*;
- through what other characters say about them;
- through what they do, their actions.

As you read the play, examine the following scenes for what they reveal about Banquo's character and fill in the chart briefly using your own words. If you need more room, use the back of the page.

Scene	What Banquo says, does or what others say about him	What this reveals about Banquo's character
Act I, scene iii Macbeth and Banquo meet the three witches		
Act I, scene iii Ross and Angus tell Macbeth about his new title		
Act I, scene iv Duncan thanks Banquo for his loyalty and bravery		
Act I, scene vi Duncan arrives at Macbeth's castle		

© 1994 by The Center for Applied Research in Education

NAME:_____   DATE:_____

During-reading Activity
for
Macbeth
Guide to Character Development: Ross
Act I

Shakespeare reveals his characters in four ways:

- ❧ through what the characters say to other characters in dialogue;
- ❧ through what the characters reveal about their thoughts through long speeches to the audience called *soliloquies*;
- ❧ through what other characters say about them;
- ❧ through what they do, their actions.

As you read the play, examine the following scenes for what they reveal about Ross's character and fill in the chart briefly using your own words. If you need more room, use the back of the page.

Scene	*What Ross says, does or what others say about him*	*What this reveals about Ross's character*
Act I, scene ii The Captain's description of Macbeth during the battle and Duncan's response		
Act I, scene iii Ross and Angus tell Macbeth about his new title		

**During-reading Activity
for
Macbeth
Guide to Character Development: Malcolm
*Act I***

Shakespeare reveals his characters in four ways:

- through what the characters say to other characters in dialogue;
- through what the characters reveal about their thoughts through long speeches to the audience called *soliloquies*;
- through what other characters say about them;
- through what they do, their actions.

As you read the play, examine the following scenes for what they reveal about Malcolm's character and fill in the chart briefly using your own words. If you need more room, use the back of the page.

Scene	*What Malcolm says, does or what others say about him*	*What this reveals about Malcolm's character*
Act I, scene ii The Captain's description of Macbeth during the battle and Duncan's response		
Act I, scene iv Duncan names Malcolm Prince of Cumberland		

NAME:_____   DATE:_____

During-reading Activity
for
Macbeth
Guide to Character Development: The Witches
Act I

Shakespeare reveals his characters in four ways:

- through what the characters say to other characters in dialogue;
- through what the characters reveal about their thoughts through long speeches to the audience called *soliloquies*;
- through what other characters say about them;
- through what they do, their actions.

As you read the play, examine the following scenes for what they reveal about the witches' characters and fill in the chart briefly using your own words. If you need more room, use the back of the page.

Scene	What the witches say, do or what others say about them	What this reveals about the witches' characters
Act I, scene i Witches agree to meet with Macbeth		
Act I, scene iii Macbeth and Banquo meet the three witches		

Postreading Activity
for
Macbeth
Comprehension Check
Act I

Directions: After you've read all of Act I, use the following questions to check how well you've understood what you've read. For each question, select the most appropriate answer from the choices listed below it. Place the letter corresponding to your answer in the space to the left of the item number.

____1.   How does Duncan reward Macbeth for his valor?

A. Grants him title Thane of Glamis.
B. Grants him title Thane of Fife.
C. Grants him title Thane of Cawdor.
D. Grants him title Thane of Ross.
E. Grants him title Thane of Menteith.

____2.   In Macbeth's letter to his wife, he wishes to share the news of the prophecy of his becoming king with his wife. What is her response to the promise of kingship?

A. That she'll wait for the future patiently.
B. That she'll urge her husband to overcome all hurdles to become king.
C. That she'll take care of any and all hurdles so that he can become king.
D. That she'll murder Duncan herself if he can't bring himself to do it.
E. That she'll poison the king's dinner while no one is looking.

____3.   Macbeth responds to Duncan's naming Malcolm Prince of Cumberland with these lines:

❧

The Prince of Cumberland—that is a step,
On which I must fall down, or else o'er leap,
For in my way it lies.

❧

These lines suggest that

A. Macbeth views Malcolm as a major threat to becoming king.
B. Macbeth needs to murder Malcolm first.
C. Macbeth views Malcolm as a minor obstacle to becoming king.
D. Macbeth plans to poison Malcolm.
E. Malcolm is more powerful than Macbeth.

___4. When Lady Macbeth learns that Duncan will spend the night at Inverness, she

A. recognizes it as the perfect opportunity to murder Duncan.
B. recognizes it as the wrong time to murder Duncan.
C. is angry because she is unprepared.
D. recognizes it as an opportunity to eliminate Malcolm.
E. plans to poison both Duncan and Malcolm.

___5. How does Macbeth's initial response to the prophecy of becoming king differ from Lady Macbeth's?

A. Macbeth wants to become king immediately; Lady Macbeth wants him to wait.
B. Macbeth doesn't know how he will succeed Duncan; Lady Macbeth wants to eliminate any barrier.
C. Macbeth plans to murder Duncan; Lady Macbeth wants to wait.
D. Macbeth plans to murder Malcolm and wait for Duncan to die; Lady Macbeth plans to murder both.
E. Macbeth plans a revolt to overthrow Duncan; Lady Macbeth wants a quiet murder.

NAME:_____   DATE: _____

Postreading Activity
for
Macbeth
Small Group Discussion to Check Comprehension
Act I

Directions: After you've read all of Act I, discuss each of the following questions in small groups briefly. Use the space below each question to note points you may want to share later. If you need more room, use the back of the page.

1. What sequence of events lead Duncan to name Macbeth Thane of Cawdor?

2. What is Lady Macbeth's response to the prophecy that Macbeth will become king?

3. How might Duncan's naming Malcolm Prince of Cumberland interfere with Macbeth's becoming king?

4. What is Lady Macbeth's reaction to finding out that Duncan is coming to Inverness?

5. In what ways is Macbeth's response to the prophecy of becoming king different from Lady Macbeth's?

NAME:_____   DATE: _____

Postreading Activity
for
Macbeth
Critical Thinking Questions
Act I

Directions: To help you develop your understanding of Act I, as your teacher directs you, take time to think about and discuss the following questions. The first question is the focus question and is the point of the discussion. Don't be concerned that you may not be able to answer this question at first. Proceed to the exploration questions and then return to the focus question.

Focus Question. If you were Macbeth, what would you be willing to do to help fulfill the witches' prophecy of becoming king?

Exploration Questions.

1. What outside forces do you feel often control your life?

2. How do people today feel about destiny or fate controlling their lives?

3. How do Macbeth, Lady Macbeth, and Banquo differ in their acceptance of the witches' prophecies?

4. If you were Macbeth, how might you react initially to the witches' prophecies? How might you react once Angus and Ross informed you of your new title, Thane of Cawdor?

• 5. Compare and contrast the role of destiny or fate upon Macbeth with that of a character from another work of literature.

6. What characters, situations, or actions in other works of literature confirm your belief or disbelief about the "existence" of destiny or fate?

Postreading Activity
for
Macbeth
Language Exploration
Figurative Language—Simile and Metaphor
Act I

As other poets and playwrights do, Shakespeare also explores abstract ideas such as revenge, personal honor, and sacrificing personal goals for public ones in his plays. He often connects abstract ideas with concrete examples through the use of *figurative language*. Although we rarely mean figurative language in a literal sense, it does help us express our ideas more vividly. Two common literary devices associated with figurative language are *simile* and *metaphor*.

A *simile* compares two different terms using *like* or *as*. In daily speech we often use similes like these:

ɞ

Sam is <u>as hungry as a bear</u>.
Angel runs <u>like the wind</u>

ɞ

Similarly, in one of the early scenes of *Macbeth*, the captain uses a simile to describe the battle between the rebellious Macdonwald and Duncan's armies (Act I, scene ii):

ɞ

<u>Doubtful it stood</u>,
<u>As two spent swimmers</u>, that do cling together
And choke their art.

ɞ

Here, the captain compares the battle-weary armies to two tired swimmers. The swimmers cling to each other to keep from drowning, suggesting that the soldiers don't fight well because they are fatigued.

Another way to compare two different terms is to use a *metaphor*. Unlike a simile, a metaphor makes a direct comparison without using *like* or *as*. As metaphors, the previous examples look like this:

৯৯

Sam is a real bear when he's hungry.
Angel breezed across the finish line.

৯৯

Banquo uses a metaphor when he asks the witches about what prophecies they may have for him (Act I, scene iii):

৯৯

. . . To me you speak not.
If you can look into the seeds of time,
And say which grain will grow, and which will not,
Speak then to me , . . .

৯৯

The metaphor here compares future events to seeds or kernels of grain. Banquo wishes to know the events, like the kernels that sprout, that will be fruitful for him.

Directions: The following passages contain examples of *simile* and *metaphor*. Working in pairs, small groups, or as your teacher directs, identify the comparisons and then review each passage within the context of the play to develop an interpretation of the passage. You may want to review the quotations within the fuller context of a particular speech.

1. Banquo commenting on the sudden disappearance of the witches (Act I, scene iii):

৯৯

The earth hath bubbles, as the water has,
And these are of them. Wither are they vanished?

৯৯

2. Macbeth's response to Banquo's question (Act I, scene iii):

৯৯

Into the air; and what seemed corporal melted,
As breath into the wind. Would they had stayed.

৯৯

57

3. Macbeth responding to the news that he's now Thane of Cawdor (Act I, scene iii):

❧

> *Two truths are told,*
> *As happy prologues to the swelling act*
> *Of the imperial theme.*

❧

4. Macbeth responding to Ross and Angus' efforts to find him (Act I, scene iii):

❧

> *. . . Kind gentlemen, your pains*
> *Are registered where every day I turn*
> *The leaf to read them.*

❧

5. Duncan welcoming Macbeth to his court (Act I, scene iv):

❧

> *Welcome hither.*
> *I have begun to plant thee, and will labor*
> *To make thee full of growing.*

❧

6. Macbeth contemplating Duncan's decision to name Malcolm Prince of Cumberland and heir to the Scottish throne (Act I, scene iv):

❧

> *The Prince of Cumberland—that is a step,*
> *On which I must fall down, or else o'er leap,*
> *For in my way it lies.*

❧

© 1994 by The Center for Applied Research in Education

7. Duncan commenting on Macbeth's character to Banquo (Act I, scene iv):

&

True worthy Banquo—he is full so valiant,
And in his commendations I am fed.
It is a banquet to me.

&

8. Lady Macbeth commenting to Macbeth (Act I, scene v):

&

Your face, my Thane, is as a book, where men
May read strange matters.

&

9. Lady Macbeth instructing her husband (Act I, scene v):

&

. . . To beguile the time,
Look like the time; bear welcome in your eye,
Your hand, your tongue; look like the innocent flower,
But be the serpent under't.

&

10. Macbeth contemplating how the people will react to the murder of Duncan (Act I, vii):

&

The deep damnation of his taking off,
And pity, like a new-born babe,
Striding the blast, or heaven's cherubin, horsed
Upon the sightless couriers of the air,
Shall blow the horrid deed in every eye,
That tears shall drown the wind.

&

Postreading Activity
for
Macbeth
Vocabulary in Context
Act I

Directions: In each of the passages below you will find one of the words from the prereading vocabulary list for Act I. Review the definitions given in the prereading vocabulary. Working individually, in pairs, or in small groups as your teacher directs, examine each of the underlined words in the following passages from Act I. For each word, use the appropriate meaning and develop a brief interpretation of the passage within the context of the play.

1. King Duncan asking for news of the recent battle (scene ii):

    ❧

    What bloody man is that? He can report,
    As seemeth by his <u>plight</u>, of the revolt
    The newest state.

    ❧

2. Malcolm identifying the wounded captain as the one who helped free him (scene i):

    ❧

    Hail brave friend.
    Say to the King the knowledge of the <u>broil</u>
    As thou didst leave it.

    ❧

© 1994 by The Center for Applied Research in Education

3.   Captain reporting Macbeth's bravery in battle (scene ii):

&

For brave Macbeth—well he deserves that name—
<u>Disdaining</u> fortune, with his brandished steel,
.   .   .
Till he faced the slave;

&

4.   Captain describing the Norwegians' attack upon the Scottish forces (scene ii):

&

But the Norweyan lord, surveying <u>vantage</u>,
With furbished arms, and new supplies of men,
Began a fresh assault.

&

5.   Ross describing the scene at Fife (scene ii):

&

Where the Norweyan banners <u>flout</u> the sky,
And fan our people cold.

&

6.   Macbeth addressing the witches after they predict his titles (scene iii):

&

.   .   . Say from whence
You owe this strange <u>intelligence</u>, or why
Upon this blasted heath you stop our way
With such prophetic greeting?

&

7. Macbeth commenting upon the witches' sudden disappearance (scene iii):

&

Into the air; and what seemed <u>corporal</u> melted,
As breath into the wind. Would they had stayed.

&

8. Macbeth requesting leave of Duncan, so Macbeth can inform his wife of the king's visit (scene iv):

&

I'll be myself the <u>harbinger</u>, and make joyful
The hearing of my wife with your approach;
So humbly take my leave.

&

9. Macbeth recounting his experiences in a letter to Lady Macbeth (scene v):

&

When I burnt in desire to question them further, they made themselves
air, into which they vanished. Whiles I stood rapt in the wonder of it,
came missives from the king, who all-hailed me Thane of Cawdor, by
which title, before, these <u>weird</u> sisters saluted me, and referred me to the
coming on of time with, hail King that shalt be.

&

10. Lady Macbeth vowing to help her husband become king (scene v):

&

. . . Hie thee hither,
That I may pour my spirits in thine ear,
And chastise with the valour of my tongue
All that <u>impedes</u> thee from the golden round,

&

NAME:_____   DATE:_____

Vocabulary Review Quiz
for
Macbeth
Act I

Directions: For each of the italicized words in the sentences below, determine which letter best reflects the use of the word in this context. Place the letter corresponding to your answer in the space to the left of the item number.

____1.   When Duncan mentions the captain's *plight*, he is referring to

A. his sense of humor   B. his valor   C. his cowardice   D. his wounds
E. his helpfulness

____2.   When Malcolm says that the soldier had knowledge of the *broil*, he was referring to

A. cooking   B. the branding of traitors   C. the desire for vengeance
D. the campfire   E. the recent battle

____3.   To say that Macbeth *disdained* fortune suggests that Macbeth fought

A. with no thought of personal gain.   B. with only cowardly intentions of personal safety.   C. with care not to be injured.   D. with skill to protect his army.   E. for monetary gain.

____4.   The Norwegian army attacked after surveying *vantage* suggests that the Norwegians

A. felt that they would lose but wanted to die trying.   B. felt they could benefit from their present military position.   C. wanted to retreat.
D. wanted to forget about taking Scotland and go home.   E. wanted to find an escape route to the sea.

____5.   When Ross says the Norwegian banners *flout* the sky, he is suggesting that

A. the banners look pretty.   B. the banners, like their owners, are large.   C. the Norwegian banners seem to mock the Scottish people in the surrounding area.   D. the Norwegians are retreating.   E. the Norwegian forces will soon be victorious in Fife.

____6.   When Macbeth asks the witches how they come by their *intelligence*, he means

A. how did they learn witchcraft.   B. how smart they are.   C. they are spies for the Norwegian forces.   D. where and how have they come to know the prophecies.   E. when will they be able to tell him more.

____7.   When Macbeth thought the witches were *corporal* beings, he thought
A. they were mortal.   B. they were divine.   C. they were powerful.
D. they were magical.   E. they were strange.

____8.   When Macbeth offers to make himself Duncan's *harbinger*, he is offering
to

A. spy for the King.   B. announce the king's arrival at Inverness.
C. raise an army for the king.   D. secure fresh horses.   E. escort the
King home.

____9.   When Macbeth refers to the witches, he often calls them *weird* sisters,
suggesting that

A. they are ugly.   B. they are extremely odd.   C. they may influence
his fate.   D. they are unknown to him.   E. they are his protectors.

____10.   When Lady Macbeth promises to help her husband conquer anything
that *impedes* his becoming king, she suggests that

A. Macbeth has a speech problem.   B. Macbeth is a fool.   C. she'll help
him overcome any barrier.   D. he is unable and unfit to rule.   E. Macbeth
is destined to become king.

ACT II

Focusing Activities
for
Macbeth
Scenarios for Improvisation
Act II

Directions: Presented below are locations and situations involving characters. As your teacher directs you, and before reading an individual scene, pretend to be one of the characters and act out the situation. Don't worry about speaking like the characters in Shakespeare's plays, just try to imagine how you would react to the situation and use your own language. Your teacher may give you a few minutes to discuss what you would like to do with the other performers. Your teacher will probably ask you to act out your scene for others in the class. When you finish, your teacher may ask your classmates to discuss what they've seen.

scene i.   *Scene*: Macbeth's castle in the early hours of the morning.

Characters: Macbeth and Banquo.

Situation: Macbeth is on his way to murder Duncan. He accidentally meets Banquo. Improvise the scene between them.

scene ii.   *Scene*: Macbeth's castle.

Characters: Lady Macbeth and Macbeth.

Situation: Macbeth, horrified that he's murdered Duncan, brings the bloody daggers with him from the chamber. Improvise the scene.

scene iv.   *Scene*: A peasant cottage near Inverness.

Characters: A peasant farmer and his wife.

Situation: On a recent trip to market, the wife learns of the death of Duncan and returns to tell her husband. Improvise the scene between them.

Focusing Activities
for
Macbeth
Small Group Discussion Questions
Act II

Directions: Before reading the scenes in Act II, discuss the questions in small groups. You may want to make notes about your discussion so you can share them with classmates or refer back to them after you've read the scene.

scenes i and ii. Although Lady Macbeth has reconvinced her husband that he should kill Duncan, what do you think might prevent them from being successful?

scenes iii and iv. How do you think the other nobles will react when they learn that Duncan has been murdered? How do you think his sons Malcolm and Donalbain will react? Macbeth? Lady Macbeth? The common people of Scotland?

Focusing Activities
for
Macbeth
Speculation Journal
Act II

Directions: This activity is to help you become involved actively with reading the play by helping you to determine a definite purpose for reading. Before you read these scenes in Act II, take a few minutes to respond in writing to the questions below. Don't worry about correct answers here. Use your own experience, what you know, or what you may have heard about the play to speculate about what you think might happen. After reading a scene, you may find that the characters reacted differently than you thought. Don't worry about these differences; just make note of them because you will have opportunities to share these differences in other activities.

scenes i and ii. Pretend to be either Macbeth or Lady Macbeth and write a brief diary entry before reading further. What might you fear that would keep your plans to murder Duncan from succeeding?

scenes iii and iv. How do you think the other nobles will react when they learn that Duncan has been murdered? How do you think Duncan's sons Malcolm and Donalbain will react? Macbeth? Lady Macbeth? The common people of Scotland?

After reading Act II: Now that you have finished reading Act II, which of your speculations were most accurate? How do you account for them? Which ones were least like the action of the play? Why do you think you speculated as you did?

Prereading Activity
for
Macbeth
Vocabulary
Act II

Directions: Shakespeare uses the following words in Act II. The section below provides a brief definition of each word and provides a sentence to illustrate its meaning. You may wish to review the words for a particular scene immediately before reading it.

Definitions.

scene i

1. **husbandry:** (n.) careful, thrifty management of domestic resources.
   Example: My grandmother's *husbandry* of her household accounts allowed her to take many extensive trips to Europe.

2. **summons:** (n.) a request, demand, call to duty, task, or performance.
   Example: Making only a <u>B</u> on the first calculus test was a *summons* to Jennifer to work harder in preparing for the next one.

3. **franchise:** (v.) to make or set free.
   Example: Trusting in the defendant's innocence *franchised* the attorney to work harder to win on appeal.

4. **palpable:** (adj.) plainly visible; tangible.
   Example: When we returned home, we found broken pieces of the lamp on the floor: *palpable* evidence of the cat's guilt.

5. **marshal:** (v.) to usher or lead.
   Example: As a school crossing guard, my grandfather *marshals* small children across busy city streets.

scene ii

6. **surfeit:** (v.) to eat or drink excessively.
   Example: The politician, *surfeited* from too much wine and dinner, snored loudly while his opponent addressed the guests at the banquet.

7. **contend:** (v.) to struggle; oppose.
   Example: Although Enid *contended* an incumbent, she won the election on issues.

© 1994 by The Center for Applied Research in Education

scene iii

8. **clamor:** (v.) to make loud noises; to drive, force, influence noisily.
   Example: The sold-out crowd *clamored* for the rock star to begin the concert.

9. **badge:** (v.) to furnish or mark with a badge.
   Example: Bruises and sprains *badged* the football team for the weeks following their championship game.

scene iv

10. **benison:** (n.) benediction.
    Example: When we left my friend John's house, his wry *benison* was to "go in pieces."

Prereading Activity
for
Macbeth
Plot Summaries
Act II

Directions: To help you better understand and follow *Macbeth*, read the summary of a specific scene before you begin to read it. If you get lost during the scene, you can refer to the summary.

Act II,
scene i

In the castle later that evening, Banquo enters with his son Fleance. They establish that it is past midnight and the stars and the moon seem to have gone out. When Macbeth enters, Banquo at first reaches for his sword to protect himself and the king from harm.

Realizing that it is Macbeth, Banquo resheathes his sword. Banquo tells Macbeth about his dream of the three witches and would like to talk with Macbeth about it some more. Banquo leaves. Macbeth then tells his servant to go to Lady Macbeth and have her strike the bell when his drink is ready.

In his soliloquy, Macbeth's vision of the dagger foreshadows the murder of Duncan. Macbeth sees a dagger with its handle towards him. He questions whether it is real or not. The dagger seems to draw Macbeth towards the chamber where King Duncan sleeps. The dagger now seems to be covered with blood. Macbeth then comments that the time is one when mortals sleep but evil and witchcraft are abroad. Macbeth then hopes that the living don't hear him as he stalks Duncan. When the bell sounds inside, he knows that the plan is set: He goes to murder Duncan.

Act II,
scene ii

Outside Duncan's chambers, Lady Macbeth has drugged the king's guards, so they will not see Macbeth enter or hear the king cry out. She has also taken their daggers from them for her husband to use as the murder weapons. Macbeth hears her and startles them both.

Macbeth returns with the bloody daggers. He recounts that one of the guards laughed in his sleep while the other cried "murder!" and woke them both. While Macbeth hid in the dark, the guards said prayers and went back to sleep. Macbeth is upset that he could not pronounce the Amen with them at the end of their prayers.

© 1994 by The Center for Applied Research in Education

Lady Macbeth tells him not to worry about it. She takes the daggers from Macbeth and urges him to go wash the blood from his hands. She will take the daggers back to the guards and smear them with the king's blood, so that they will receive the blame. Someone begins to knock on the gate, rousing the household. Lady Macbeth urges her husband to change into his night clothes, so it will appear that he has been asleep.

Act II, scene iii

At the castle gate, the knocking grows louder. The drunken porter finally answers the gate. Macduff and Lennox have come to escort King Duncan as he has ordered. Macbeth enters. They ask if Duncan is up yet. Macbeth shows Macduff to Duncan's chamber. While Macduff goes to rouse the king, Lennox informs Macbeth that there was a violent storm during the night: chimneys were blown down, strange cries of death were heard, some even rumored of earthquakes.

Macduff discovers the body and rouses the rest of the household. When Malcolm and Donalbain, Duncan's sons, enter, they decide that they need to flee to avoid being named as the murderers or the next victims. Malcolm goes to England and Donalbain to Ireland.

Act II, scene iv

In the world outside the castle, Ross and the old man discuss the strange things that have happened in the world. The old man points to omens of unnatural occurrences—a solar eclipse occurs; an owl has killed a falcon. Ross reports that Duncan's horses went wild.

Macduff enters and reports that Macbeth has slain the guards everyone suspects murdered the king. He also reports that Duncan's sons have fled, making them likely conspirators. With no clear successor to the throne, Macbeth has been named king and has already gone to Scone to be crowned.

Class Period:

CHARACTER ASSIGNMENTS FOR ORAL READING GROUPS
Macbeth

Session 3: Act II, scenes i, ii, iii, iv

Characters	Group 1	Group 2	Group 3	Group 4
Banquo	_____	_____	_____	_____
Fleance, Donalbain	_____	_____	_____	_____
Macbeth	_____	_____	_____	_____
Lady Macbeth	_____	_____	_____	_____
Porter	_____	_____	_____	_____
Macduff	_____	_____	_____	_____
Lennox, Old Man	_____	_____	_____	_____
Malcolm, Ross	_____	_____	_____	_____

74

NAME:_____   DATE:_____

During-reading Activity
for
Macbeth
Character Diary 3
Act II, scenes i, ii, iii, iv

Directions: Use the space below to record your character's reactions to the events of the four scenes in Act II of *Macbeth*. Remember to include a summary of events, explain how your character learned of them, and give your character's reactions to them. Because this act has four scenes, you may want to record your character's entries as you read each scene. If you need additional room, use the back of this sheet.

The Personal Diary of

_____
(character's name)

Inverness
The next day

_____
_____
_____
_____
_____
_____
_____
_____
_____
_____
_____
_____
_____
_____
_____
_____

During-reading Activity
for
Macbeth
Viewing Act II, scene ii
Macbeth and Lady Macbeth React to Murdering Duncan

Directions: After you've read this scene, viewing a film or video version may help you better understand how the text translates into the characters' actions. Although you may want to keep your copy of the play handy, don't be surprised if the actors' script varies from yours. Film scripts often delete or reorder the lines in the play. You many want to note questions you need to ask your teacher afterwards. After viewing the scene, take a few minutes to respond to the questions below.

1. Based upon what you've seen, how do Macbeth and Lady Macbeth react differently to murdering King Duncan?

2. Based upon what you've seen, why do you think Macbeth and Lady Macbeth react differently to murdering Duncan?

During-reading Activity
for
Macbeth
Guide to Character Development: Macbeth
Act II

Shakespeare reveals his characters in four ways:

- through what the characters say to other characters in dialogue;
- through what the characters reveal about their thoughts through long speeches to the audience called *soliloquies*;
- through what other characters say about them;
- through what they do, their actions.

As you read the play, examine the following scenes for what they reveal about Macbeth's character and fill in the chart briefly using your own words. If you need more room, use the back of the page.

Scene	What Macbeth says, does, or what others say about him	What this reveals about Macbeth's character
Act II, scene i On the way to Duncan's chamber, Macbeth meets Banquo		
Act II, scene i Macbeth's soliloquy ("Is this a dagger which I see before me")		
Act II, scene ii Macbeth and Lady Macbeth meet after Macbeth has murdered Duncan		
Act II, scene ii Someone is knocking at the gate		

Act II, scene iii Macduff and Lennox come to escort Duncan		
Act II, scene iv Macduff discovers Duncan's body		

© 1994 by The Center for Applied Research in Education

NAME:_____   DATE:_____

During-reading Activity
for
Macbeth
Guide to Character Development: Lady Macbeth
Act II

Shakespeare reveals his characters in four ways:

- ❧ through what the characters say to other characters in dialogue;
- ❧ through what the characters reveal about their thoughts through long speeches to the audience called *soliloquies*;
- ❧ through what other characters say about them;
- ❧ through what they do, their actions.

As you read the play, examine the following scenes for what they reveal about Lady Macbeth's character and fill in the chart briefly using your own words. If you need more room, use the back of the page.

Scene	*What Lady Macbeth says, does, or what others say about her*	*What this reveals about Lady Macbeth's character*
Act II, scene ii Macbeth and Lady Macbeth meet after Macbeth has murdered Duncan		
Act II, scene ii Someone is knocking at the gate		
Act II, scene iii Macduff and Lennox come to escort Duncan		
Act II, scene iv Macduff discovers Duncan's body		

79

**During-reading Activity
for
Macbeth
Guide to Character Development: Banquo
*Act II***

Shakespeare reveals his characters in four ways:

- through what the characters say to other characters in dialogue;
- through what the characters reveal about their thoughts through long speeches to the audience called *soliloquies*;
- through what other characters say about them;
- through what they do, their actions.

As you read the play, examine the following scenes for what they reveal about Banquo's character and fill in the chart briefly using your own words. If you need more room, use the back of the page.

Scene	What Banquo says, does, or what others say about him	What this reveals about Banquo's character
Act II, scene i On the way to Duncan's chamber, Macbeth meets Banquo		
Act II, scene iv Macduff discovers Duncan's body		

© 1994 by The Center for Applied Research in Education

NAME:_____   DATE:_____

During-reading Activity
for
Macbeth
Guide to Character Development: Macduff
Act II

Shakespeare reveals his characters in four ways:

- ✒ through what the characters say to other characters in dialogue;
- ✒ through what the characters reveal about their thoughts through long speeches to the audience called *soliloquies*;
- ✒ through what other characters say about them;
- ✒ through what they do, their actions.

As you read the play, examine the following scenes for what they reveal about Macduff's character and fill in the chart briefly using your own words. If you need more room, use the back of the page.

Scene	*What Macduff says, does, or what others say about him*	*What this reveals about Macduff's character*
Act II, scene iv Macduff discovers Duncan's body		
Act II, scene v Malcolm and Donalbain flee and Macbeth is named king		

During-reading Activity
for
Macbeth
Guide to Character Development: Ross
Act II

Shakespeare reveals his characters in four ways:

🙠 through what the characters say to other characters in dialogue;

🙠 through what the characters reveal about their thoughts through long speeches to the audience called *soliloquies*;

🙠 through what other characters say about them;

🙠 through what they do, their actions.

As you read the play, examine the following scenes for what they reveal about Ross's character and fill in the chart briefly using your own words. If you need more room, use the back of the page.

Scene	What Ross says, does, or what others say about him	What this reveals about Ross's character
Act II, scene iv Ross and the old man discuss the murder of Duncan and its effects		

During-reading Activity
for
Macbeth
Guide to Character Development: Malcolm
Act II

Shakespeare reveals his characters in four ways:

- 🙠 through what the characters say to other characters in dialogue;
- 🙠 through what the characters reveal about their thoughts through long speeches to the audience called *soliloquies*;
- 🙠 through what other characters say about them;
- 🙠 through what they do, their actions.

As you read the play, examine the following scenes for what they reveal about Malcolm's character and fill in the chart briefly using your own words. If you need more room, use the back of the page.

Scene	What Malcolm says, does, or what others say about him	What this reveals about Malcolm's character
Act II, scene iii Macduff discovers Duncan's body		
Act II, scene iv Malcolm and Donalbain flee		

NAME:_____   DATE:_____

Postreading Activity
for
Macbeth
Comprehension Check
Act II

Directions: After you've read all of Act II, use the following questions to check how well you've understood what you've read. For each question, select the most appropriate answer from the choices listed below it. Place the letter corresponding to your answer in the space to the left of the item number.

_____1.   How does Lady Macbeth assist in the murdering of Duncan?

A. She puts poison on the knife blades.
B. She kills Malcolm while Macbeth stabs Duncan.
C. She drugs the guards.
D. She drugs the gate porter.
E. She kills Donalbain.

_____2.   Why do Macduff and Lennox come to Inverness?

A. They suspect Duncan is in danger.
B. They have a favor to ask of the king.
C. They suspect Macbeth may murder the king.
D. They've come to kill Duncan.
E. They've come to escort the king.

_____3.   What do the following lines, spoken by Macbeth after he's murdered Duncan, suggest about his character?

ᔑ

Still it cried, sleep no more, to all the house.
Glamis has murdered sleep, and therefore Cawdor
Shall sleep no more. Macbeth shall sleep no more.

ᔑ

© 1994 by The Center for Applied Research in Education

A. That Macbeth is an insomniac.
B. That Macbeth's guilt will always be with him.
C. That he shouldn't have listened to his wife.
D. That he's sorry for what he's done.
E. That he can now become the rightful king.

_____4.   What is the significance of Lennox's description of the events of the night before he and Macduff arrive at Inverness?

ᢓ

The night has been unruly. Where we lay,
Our chimneys were blown down, and as they say,
Lamentings heard i' th' air, strange screams of death,
And prophesying, with accents terrible,
Of dire combustion, and confused events,
New hatched to th' woeful time.

ᢓ

A. That there was a bad storm.
B. That Lennox has an overly active imagination.
C. That the witches tried to catch Lennox and Macduff.
D. That something has disrupted the order of the world.
E. That Duncan has changed his mind about making Malcolm his heir.

_____5.   Which of the following is not a reason for the nobles to believe that Malcolm is responsible for the murder of Duncan?

A. Donalbain flees to Ireland.
B. The guards are blood-stained.
C. Malcolm flees to England.
D. The guards were found holding the weapons.
E. Duncan was murdered before Malcolm was formally invested as Prince of Cumberland.

Postreading Activity
for
Macbeth
Small Group Discussion to Check Comprehension
Act II

Directions: After you've read all of Act II, discuss each of the following questions in small groups briefly. Use the space below each question to note points you may want to share later. If you need more room, use the back of the page.

1.   What does Lady Macbeth do to assist in the murdering of the king?

2.   Why do Lennox and Macduff come knocking at the gate so early?

3.   What does Macbeth do or say after murdering Duncan that suggests he may regret his actions?

4.   Besides the discovery and description of the body, what other events are reported during the act that reflect the enormity of the murder?

5.   How does Macbeth deliberately misinterpret the evidence surrounding the murder of Duncan, so that he can become king?

Postreading Activity
for
Macbeth
Critical Thinking Questions
Act II

Directions: To help you develop your understanding of Act II, as your teacher directs you, take time to think about and discuss the following questions. The first question is the focus question and is the point of the discussion. Don't be concerned that you may not be able to answer this question at first. Proceed to the exploration questions and then return to the focus question.

Focus Question. How do you, as a member of contemporary society, react differently to Macbeth's murdering of Duncan than either he or Lady Macbeth do?

Exploration Questions.

1. How have you responded when you learned that you or someone else was going to receive an unearned reward?

2. How do Macbeth and the other nobles react to the killing of Duncan, whom they regard as the divinely ordained and rightful king?

3. In other works of literature, how have characters cheated the system to get what they wanted?

4. How would you react differently from these characters of other works, in similar situations?

5. If you were either Macbeth or Lady Macbeth, why would you feel justified in murdering Duncan?

6. Why do you think the characters within *Macbeth* are more horrified at the idea of murdering a king than we are about political assassinations in our society?

Postreading Activity
for
Macbeth
Language Exploration
Figurative Language: Personification and Apostrophe
Act II

We have seen how Shakespeare uses *simile* and *metaphor* to develop figurative language. Like Shakespeare, we also use other devices to express abstract ideas more concretely, among them *personification* and *apostrophe*.

We use *personification* to give human characteristics to inanimate or nonhuman things. We may say that "Love is blind," or argue with the soft drink machine that "eats" our change. In Act I, scene ii, the Captain personifies Macbeth's sword (brandished steel) and suggests that it acted on its own to bring Macbeth face to face with Macdonwald:

Disdaining fortune, with his brandished steel,
Which smoked with bloody execution,
Like valor's minion carved out his passage
Till he faced the slave;

Another figurative device is to address a person or abstract idea directly although it is not or cannot be present. This device is called *apostrophe*. The following expressions are examples:

Death, be not proud.

or

Twinkle, twinkle little star,
How I wonder what you are?

When Lady Macbeth learns that Duncan is coming to Inverness and that she'll have her opportunity to murder the king, she addresses spirits using an apostrophe (Act I, scene v):

❧

> *. . . Come you spirits*
> *That tend mortal thoughts, unsex me here,*
> *And fill me from crown to the toe top-full*
> *Of direst cruelty!*

❧

Directions: The following passages contain examples of personification and apostrophe. Working in pairs, small groups, or as your teacher directs, review each passage within the context of the play and develop an interpretation of the passage. You may want to review the quotations within the fuller context of a particular speech.

1. Ross describing the Norwegian banners flying from the battlements of the castle at Fife (Act I, scene ii):

❧

> *From Fife, great King,*
> *Where Norweyan banners flout the sky*
> *And fan our people cold.*

❧

2. Angus relating the downfall of the former Thane of Cawdor (Act I, scene iii):

❧

> *But treasons capital, confessed and proved,*
> *Have overthrown him.*

❧

3.   Lady Macbeth learning that Duncan comes to Inverness (Act I, scene v):

ès

> *. . . Come thick night,*
> *And pall thee in the dunnest smoke of hell,*
> *That my keen knife see not the wound it makes,*
> *Nor heaven peep through the blanket of the dark,*
> *To cry, hold, hold!*

ès

4.   Banquo describing Inverness castle to Duncan (Act I, scene vi):

ès

> *This guest of summer,*
> *The temple-haunting martlet, does approve,*
> *By his loved mansionry, that the heaven's breath*
> *Smells wooingly here.*

ès

5.   Lady Macbeth to her husband (Act I, scene vii):

ès

> *Was the hope drunk,*
> *Wherein you dressed yourself? Hath it slept since?*
> *And wakes it now to look so green and pale,*
> *At what it did so freely?*

ès

6.   Banquo contemplating the witches' prophecies (Act II, scene i):

❧

> *. . . Merciful powers,*
> *Restrain in me the cursed thoughts that nature*
> *Gives way to in repose*

❧

7.   Macbeth on his way to murder Duncan (Act II, scene i):

❧

> *I go and it is done. The bell invites me.*
> *Hear it not Duncan, for it is a knell*
> *That summons thee to heaven, or to hell.*

❧

8.   Macbeth going to bed after the murder but hearing the knocking at the gate (Act II, scene ii):

❧

> *Wake Duncan with thy knocking. I would thou couldst.*

❧

9.   Macduff informing others of the murder (Act II, scene iii):

❧

> *Confusion now hath made his masterpiece!*

❧

10. Ross describing the solar eclipse (Act II, scene iv):

ᛒ

Ha, good father,
Thou seest the heavens, as troubled with man's act,
Threatens his blood stage: by the clock 'tis day,
And yet dark night strangles the traveling lamp.

ᛒ

NAME:_____   DATE: _____

Postreading Activity
for
Macbeth
Vocabulary in Context
Act II

Directions: In each of the passages below you will find one of the words from the prereading vocabulary list for Act II. Review the definitions given in the prereading vocabulary. Working individually, in pairs, or in small groups as your teacher directs, examine each of the underlined words in the following passages from Act II. For each word, use the appropriate meaning and develop a brief interpretation of the passage within the context of the play.

1.   Banquo to his son Fleance, commenting upon the late night (scene i):

ॐ

. . . *There's <u>husbandry</u> in heaven,*
Their candles are all out.

ॐ

2.   Banquo commenting upon the witches' prophecies (scene i):

ॐ

A heavy <u>summons</u> lies like lead upon me,
And yet I would not sleep.

ॐ

3.   Banquo requesting time to discuss the witches' prophecies with Macbeth further (scene i):

ॐ

So I lose none
In seeking to augment it, but still keep
My bosom <u>franchised</u>, all allegiance clear,
I shall be counselled.

ॐ

4. Macbeth describing the vision of the dagger (scene i):

❧

I see thee yet, in form as <u>palpable</u>
As this which now I draw.

❧

5. Macbeth addressing the vision of the dagger (scene i):

❧

Thou <u>marshall'st</u> me the way that I was going,
And such an instrument I was to use.

❧

6. Lady Macbeth describing her preparations to assist with the murder (scene ii):

❧

The doors are open; and the <u>surfeited</u> grooms
Do mock their charge with snores.

❧

7. Lady Macbeth describing additional precautions she's taken with the guards to assist in the murder (scene ii):

❧

. . . I have drugged their possets,
That death and nature do <u>contend</u> about them,
Whether they live or die.

❧

8. Lennox describing the strange events during the night that Duncan was murdered (scene iii):

ᴈ

. . . The obscure bird
<u>Clamoured</u> the livelong night. Some say, the earth
Was feverous, and did shake.

ᴈ

9. Lennox describing the guards outside Duncan's chambers (scene iii):

ᴈ

Those of his chamber, as it seemed, had done't.
Their hands and faces were all <u>badged</u> with blood,
So were their daggers, which unwiped we found
Upon their pillows: They stared and were distracted.
No man's life was to be trusted to them.

ᴈ

10. Old man to Ross and Macduff (scene iv):

ᴈ

God's <u>benison</u> go with you, and with those
That would make good of bad, and friends of foes.

ᴈ

© 1994 by The Center for Applied Research in Education

Vocabulary Review Quiz
for
Macbeth
Act II

Directions: For each of the italicized words in the sentences below, determine which letter best reflects the use of the word in this context. Place the letter corresponding to your answer in the space to the left of the item number.

____1. For Banquo, the heaven's *husbandry* causes them to put out their candles. This image suggests that the heavens are

A. inhabited   B. disturbed   C. thrifty   D. afraid   E. lazy

____2. For Banquo, the prospect of being the father of many kings is a heavy *summons*. For him the summons is

A. an invitation   B. a demand   C. a delay   D. an omen   E. a curse

____3. Banquo sees his heart as being *franchised*; he suggests that

A. his conscience is clear   B. he is in debt to Macbeth   C. he suspects Macbeth   D. he suspects Macduff   E. he is confused

____4. Macbeth describes the dagger as *palpable*; he means it

A. appears to be real   B. appears dirty   C. appears to pulse   D. looks fake   E. looks dangerous

____5. Macbeth says that the dagger *marshals* him; he means

A. it appears to follow him   B. it disappears and reappears at will   C. it glows with a star-like light   D. it seems to lead him   E. it governs him

____6. Describing the grooms as *surfeited*, Lady Macbeth implies that

A. they're alert   B. they're dangerous   C. they're suspicious   D. they're on guard   E. they're drunk

____7. When Lady Macbeth says that death and nature *contend*, she means that they

A. honor each other   B. compete   C. struggle   D. coexist   E. make noise

___8. Lennox mentions that a bird *clamored*; he means that

A. it hatched its eggs   B. it made noise   C. it fled   D. it hunted for prey   E. it sang

___9. When the guards are described as being *badged* with blood, Lennox suggests that

A. the guards seem to wear the blood as a badge   B. in a stupor
C. seem ready to fight   D. are still asleep   E. are trustworthy

___10. The old man's *benison* is another form of

A. cure   B. benediction   C. benefit   D. curse   E. begging

ACT III

NAME:_____   DATE:_____

Focusing Activities
for
Macbeth
Scenarios for Improvisation
Act III

Directions: Presented below are locations and situations involving characters. As your teacher directs you, and before reading an individual scene, pretend to be one of the characters and act out the situation. Don't worry about speaking like the characters in Shakespeare's plays, just try to imagine how you would react to the situation and use your own language. Your teacher may give you a few minutes to discuss what you would like to do with the other performers. Your teacher will probably ask you to act out your scene for others in the class. When you finish, your teacher may ask your classmates to discuss what they've seen.

scene i. *Scene:* Macbeth and Lady Macbeth's chambers.

Characters: Macbeth and Lady Macbeth.

Situation: Macbeth and Lady Macbeth are about to make their first appearance as king and queen. You've just learned that Malcolm and Macduff have fled to England, where they have the protection of King Edward. Donalbain remains in Ireland. All refuse to admit to your version of the murder of Duncan: Malcolm and Donalbain did it. Improvise the scene between them where you plan to address this news.

scene i. *Scene:* In a hallway in the Great Hall of the Royal Palace.

Character: Banquo.

Situation: You recall that the witches made three prophecies: Macbeth would become Thane of Cawdor, Macbeth would become king, and your descendants will become kings. Improvise a soliloquy where you ponder which prophecies have come true and what this may mean for you and your descendants.

scene ii. *Scene:* Macbeth and Lady Macbeth's chambers.

Characters: Macbeth and Lady Macbeth.

Situation: Macbeth has just come from his meeting with the murderers. Remember all of Lady Macbeth's charges to be brave but concealing, like the serpent beneath the flowers. What, if anything, do you tell her about your plans for Banquo and Fleance?

scene iv. *Scene:* The banquet hall of the royal palace.

Characters: Macbeth and one of the murderers.

Situation: The murderer draws Macbeth aside and informs him that Banquo is dead but Fleance has escaped. Improvise the scene between them.

scene v. *Scene:* The witches' cavern.

Characters: The three witches and Hecate, the queen of all witches.

Situation: The three witches have been using their magic to watch what Macbeth is doing. Hecate enters and comments upon their actions. Improvise the dialogue among them.

scene vi. *Scene:* In a secluded corner of the Royal Palace.

Characters: Lords Lennox and Angus.

Situation: Both of you have witnessed Macbeth's behavior at the banquet. You now meet to discuss it. How do you interpret Macbeth and Lady Macbeth's behavior at this point?

NAME:_____   DATE:_____

Focusing Activities
for
Macbeth
Small Group Discussion Questions
Act III

Directions: Before reading the scenes in Act III, discuss the questions in small groups. You may want to make notes about your discussion so you can share them with classmates or refer back to them after you've read each scene.

scene i

1. Now that Macbeth has murdered Duncan, why do you think being king might change him? Why do you think it might change Lady Macbeth?

2. In Act I, the witches made three prophecies: Macbeth would become Thane of Cawdor, Macbeth would become king, and Banquo's descendants will become kings. If you were Banquo, how might you react to the first two coming true? What might you now think about the third prophecy that pertains to your descendants?

scene ii   If you were Macbeth, why would or wouldn't you tell Lady Macbeth about the plot to murder Banquo and Fleance?

scene iii   Why is it important to Macbeth that the murderers succeed in killing both Banquo and Fleance?

scene iv   How do you think Macbeth will respond to the news that the murderers have only partially succeeded?

scene v   If you were the queen of all witches, how might you react to the king that Macbeth has become?

scene vi   As one of the nobles of Macbeth's court, how would you react to the king that Macbeth has become?

NAME:_____   DATE:_____

Focusing Activities
for
Macbeth
Speculation Journal
Act III

Directions: This activity will help you become actively involved with reading the play by helping you to determine a definite purpose for reading. Before you read these scenes in Act III, take a few minutes to respond in writing to questions below. Don't worry about correct answers here. Use your own experience or what you have read in the play to speculate what you think will happen. After reading a scene you may find that the characters reacted differently than you thought. Don't worry about these differences; just make note of them because you will have opportunities to share these differences in other activities.

scene i

1. Now that Macbeth has murdered Duncan, how do you think being king will change him? How do you think it will change Lady Macbeth?

2. In Act I, the witches made three prophecies: Macbeth would become Thane of Cawdor, Macbeth would become king, and Banquo's descendants will become kings. How do you think Banquo will react to the first two coming true?

scene ii   If you were Macbeth, why would or wouldn't you tell Lady Macbeth about the plot to murder Banquo and Fleance?

scene iii   Why do you think that the murderers will or will not be successful in their plot to murder Banquo and Fleance?

scene iv   How do you think Macbeth will respond to the news that Banquo has been murdered? To the news that Fleance has escaped?

scene v   If you were the queen of all witches, how would you react to the king that Macbeth has become?

scene vi   As one of the nobles of Macbeth's court, how would you react to the king that Macbeth has become?

After reading Act III: Now that you have finished reading Act III, which of your speculations were most accurate? How do you account for them? Which ones were least like the action of the play? Why do you think you speculated as you did?

NAME:_____   DATE:_____

Prereading Activity
for
Macbeth
Vocabulary
Act III

Directions: Shakespeare uses the following words in Act III. The section below provides a brief definition of each word and provides a sentence to illustrate its meaning. You may want to review the words for a particular scene immediately before reading it.

Definitions.

scene i

1. **verity:** (n.) the truth; the real facts or circumstances.
   Example: One of the *verities* of politics is that leaders cannot be all things to all people.

2. **indissoluble:** (adj.) firm, stable; perpetually binding or obligatory.
   Example: In feudal times, the oaths of fealty of nobles to their kings were *indissoluble*.

3. **invention:** (n.) fabrication; fiction; plan.
   Example: The student's explanation for not doing his homework was obviously an *invention*.

4. **unlineal:** (adj.) usurped; not of direct descent or succession.
   Example: King James I became Queen Elizabeth I's *unlineal* successor, for he was a direct descendent of her grandfather Henry VII but was not her son.

5. **probation:** (n.) trial; proof.
   Example: In American courts, defendants do not need to offer *probation* of their innocence, for the court presumes their innocence.

scene ii

6. **fancy:** (n.) idea or opinion with little foundation.
   Example: Steve, my teenaged cousin, has advanced numerous *fancies* to solve his financial problems before he has thought them through.

7. **scotch:** (v.) to wound or render harmless for a time.
   Example: Ralph only *scotched* the angry hornet with the newspaper rather than kill it.

8. **sleek:** (v.) to make smooth or sleek.
   Example: Using extra fine sandpaper and steel wool, my grandfather *sleeked* the walnut table to a high gloss.

9. **seel:** (v.) to make blind; to close a person's eyes.
   Example: In Greek mythology, Odysseus and his sailors *seeled* the Cyclops with a large pointed log.

scene iv

10. **vouch:** (v.) to allege, affirm, guarantee.
    Example: When my father cosigned the loan for my first car, he *vouched* that I would make my payments.

Prereading Activity
for
Macbeth
Plot Summaries
Act III

Directions: To help you better understand and follow *Macbeth*, read the summary of a specific scene before you begin to read it. If you get lost during the scene, you can refer to the summary.

Act III, scene i

At the royal palace, Macbeth has been crowned. Banquo comments that the witches' prophecies have been fulfilled. Banquo suspects that Macbeth may have had more to do with the outcome than many suspect, but has made no attempt to expose Macbeth or separate himself from the new king. As king, Macbeth requests that Banquo fulfill a mission for him, and then return for supper.

Once Banquo is gone, Macbeth summons two assassins to murder Banquo and his son, Fleance, that evening. Macbeth has previously convinced the murderers that Banquo rather than he did them harm, so they've sworn vengeance against Banquo.

Act III, scene ii

Lady Macbeth requests a meeting with her husband. She questions his lonely brooding about what has already been done. She urges him to be bright and happy at the banquet that evening. She also urges him to honor Banquo, especially, but not worry about the prophecy that he will beget kings because he is mortal.

Macbeth doesn't tell her that he has planned to have Banquo and Fleance murdered; he feels that she can't betray a plot that she doesn't know about.

Act III, scene iii

Later that evening, Banquo and Fleance return to the palace. Before they can enter, the assassins attack, and kill Banquo, but Fleance escapes.

Act III, scene iv

During the banquet, Macbeth acts the jovial, royal host who, along with Lady Macbeth, comes down from his seat and mingles with the guests. Macbeth chastises Banquo for missing the banquet, only to have Banquo's ghost appear in Macbeth's chair both times this occurs. Only Macbeth sees the ghost and speaks to it. Lady Macbeth attempts to quiet the alarm of the guests at Macbeth's strange behavior.

When the ghost appears a third time, Lady Macbeth attempts to cover for her husband once more but fails. Lady Macbeth orders the guests to leave.

When Macbeth and Lady Macbeth are alone, Macbeth confesses that he will be avenged for the murders. He asks her how she interprets Macduff's refusal to come to the banquet. Macbeth also vows to return to the witches and have them foretell his fate. Lady Macbeth urges her husband to sleep.

Act III, scene v

Somewhere on a heath, Hecate, the queen of witches, appears and chastises the three witches for working a spell upon Macbeth's destiny without consulting her. She vows to return and confound his fate.

Act III, scene vi

At the palace, Lennox shares his thoughts with another lord. Lennox questions whether Fleance killed Banquo—and Malcolm and Donalbain killed King Duncan—as Macbeth has suggested. The lord tells Lennox that Malcolm has been well received in the English court of King Edward and that Macduff has gone to England to request the aid of King Edward to send Northumberland and Siward to overthrow Macbeth and restore the rightful monarch.

The lord reports that Macbeth sent for Macduff when the king heard of Macduff's plans. Macduff refused to come to Macbeth. The lord suspects that Macbeth will seek revenge upon Macduff.

Class Period:

CHARACTER ASSIGNMENTS FOR ORAL READING GROUPS

Macbeth

Session 4: Act III, scenes i, ii, iii

Characters	*Group 1*	*Group 2*	*Group 3*	*Group 4*
Banquo	_____	_____	_____	_____
Macbeth	_____	_____	_____	_____
Lady Macbeth	_____	_____	_____	_____
Servant	_____	_____	_____	_____
First Murderer	_____	_____	_____	_____
Second Murderer	_____	_____	_____	_____
Third Murderer	_____	_____	_____	_____
Fleance	_____	_____	_____	_____

110

Class Period:

CHARACTER ASSIGNMENTS FOR ORAL READING GROUPS
Macbeth

Session 5: Act III, scenes iv, v, vi

Characters	*Group 1*	*Group 2*	*Group 3*	*Group 4*
Macbeth	____	____	____	____
Lady Macbeth	____	____	____	____
First Murderer	____	____	____	____
Banquo's ghost	____	____	____	____
Lennox	____	____	____	____
Ross	____	____	____	____
Lord(s), First Witch	____	____	____	____
Hecate				

111

During-reading Activity
for
Macbeth
Character Diary 4
Act III, scenes i, ii, iii

Directions: Use the space below to record your character's reactions to the events of the first three scenes in Act III of *Macbeth*. Remember to include a summary of events, explain how your character learned of them, and give your character's reactions to them. Because this act has six scenes, you may want to record your character's entries as you read each scene. If you need additional room, use the back of this sheet.

The Personal Diary of

_____
(character's name)

The Royal Palace at Forres
Sometime after Macbeth's coronation

_____
_____
_____
_____
_____
_____
_____
_____
_____
_____
_____
_____
_____
_____
_____
_____

**During-reading Activity
for
Macbeth
Character Diary 5
*Act III, scenes iv, v, vi***

Directions: Use the space below to record your character's reactions to the events of the last three scenes in Act III of *Macbeth*. Remember to include a summary of events, explain how your character learned of them, and give your character's reactions to them. Because this act has six scenes, you may want to record your character's entries as you read each scene. If you need additional room, use the back of this sheet.

The Personal Diary of

_____

(character's name)

The Royal Palace at Forres
Evening

_____

_____

_____

_____

_____

_____

_____

_____

_____

_____

_____

_____

_____

During-reading Activity
for
Macbeth
Viewing Act III, scene iv
Macbeth Sees Banquo's Ghost at the Banquet

Directions: After you've read this scene, viewing a film or video version may help you better understand how the text translates into the characters' actions. Although you may want to keep your copy of the play handy, don't be surprised if the actors' script varies from yours. Film scripts often delete or reorder the lines in the play. You many want to note questions you need to ask your teacher afterwards. After viewing the scene, take a few minutes to respond to the questions below.

1. Based upon what you've seen, how do Macbeth's language and actions change as he speaks first to the guests at the banquet and then to Banquo's ghost?

2. How does the director use the camera to show Macbeth's reaction to the ghost, and how Lady Macbeth and the guests react to Macbeth's strange actions?

3. Why do you think the director has chosen to represent the ghost as it is during this scene?

During-reading Activity
for
Macbeth
Guide to Character Development: Macbeth
Act III

Shakespeare reveals his characters in four ways:

- through what the characters say to other characters in dialogue;
- through what the characters reveal about their thoughts through long speeches to the audience called *soliloquies*;
- through what other characters say about them;
- through what they do, their actions.

As you read the play, examine the following scenes for what they reveal about Macbeth's character and fill in the chart briefly using your own words. If you need more room, use the back of the page.

Scene	What Macbeth says, does, or what others say about him	What this reveals about Macbeth's character
Act III, scene i Macbeth invites Banquo to a banquet		
Act III, scene i Macbeth conspires to murder Banquo and Fleance		
Act III, scene ii Macbeth fears retribution for the murders		
Act III, scene ii Macbeth doesn't reveal his plans to murder Banquo and Fleance to Lady Macbeth		

Act III, scene iii Macbeth acts the jovial host at the banquet		
Act III, scene iii Macbeth learns that Fleance has escaped		
Act III, scene iv Macbeth sees Banquo's ghost		
Act III, scene vi Macduff refuses to come when Macbeth summons him		

NAME:_____   DATE:_____

During-reading Activity
for
Macbeth
Guide to Character Development: Lady Macbeth
Act III

Shakespeare reveals his characters in four ways:

- through what the characters say to other characters in dialogue;
- through what the characters reveal about their thoughts through long speeches to the audience called *soliloquies*;
- through what other characters say about them;
- through what they do, their actions.

As you read the play, examine the following scenes for what they reveal about Lady Macbeth's character and fill in the chart briefly using your own words. If you need more room, use the back of the page.

Scene	What Lady Macbeth says, does, or what others say about her	What this reveals about Lady Macbeth's character
Act III, scene i Macbeth invites Banquo to a banquet		
Act III, scene ii Macbeth fears retribution for the murders		
Act III, scene iii Macbeth acts the jovial host at the banquet		
Act III, scene iv Macbeth sees Banquo's ghost		

During-reading Activity
for
Macbeth
Guide to Character Development: Banquo
Act III

Shakespeare reveals his characters in four ways:

ᴥ through what the characters say to other characters in dialogue;

ᴥ through what the characters reveal about their thoughts through long speeches to the audience called *soliloquies*;

ᴥ through what other characters say about them;

ᴥ through what they do, their actions.

As you read the play, examine the following scenes for what they reveal about Banquo's character and fill in the chart briefly using your own words. If you need more room, use the back of the page.

Scene	What Banquo says, does, or what others say about him	What this reveals about Banquo's character
Act III, scene i Banquo's soliloquy		
Act III, scene ii Macbeth invites Banquo to a banquet		
Act III, scene iii Murderers attack Banquo and Fleance		
Act III, scene iv Banquo's ghost appears at the banquet		

During-reading Activity
for
Macbeth
Guide to Character Development: Ross
Act III

Shakespeare reveals his characters in four ways:

- through what the characters say to other characters in dialogue;
- through what the characters reveal about their thoughts through long speeches to the audience called *soliloquies*;
- through what other characters say about them;
- through what they do, their actions.

As you read the play, examine the following scene for what it reveals about Ross's character and fill in the chart briefly using your own words. If you need more room, use the back of the page.

Scene	What Ross says, does, or what others say about him	What this reveals about Ross's character
Act III, scene iv Banquo's ghost appears at the banquet		

During-reading Activity
for
Macbeth
Guide to Character Development: The Witches
Act III

Shakespeare reveals his characters in four ways:

🙶 through what the characters say to other characters in dialogue;
🙶 through what the characters reveal about their thoughts through long speeches to the audience called *soliloquies*;
🙶 through what other characters say about them;
🙶 through what they do, their actions.

As you read the play, examine the following scene for what it reveals about the witches' characters and fill in the chart briefly using your own words. If you need more room, use the back of the page.

Scene	What the witches say, do, or what others say about them	What this reveals about the witches' characters
Act III, scene v Witches meet with Hecate		

NAME:_____   DATE:_____

Postreading Activity
for
Macbeth
Comprehension Check
Act III

Directions: After you've read all of Act III, use the following questions to check how well you've understood what you've read. For each question, select the most appropriate answer from the choices listed below it. Place the letter corresponding to your answer in the space to the left of the item number.

_____1.   How does Macbeth convince the murderers to kill Banquo?

A. He convinces them that Banquo had wronged them.
B. He threatens to have them executed.
C. He bribes them.
D. He orders them.
E. He convinces them that Banquo murdered Duncan.

_____2.   What is Macbeth's motive for having Banquo murdered?

A. To avenge Duncan's death.
B. To blame Banquo for Duncan's murder.
C. To prevent the prophecy about Banquo's heirs becoming king from coming true.
D. To avenge an insult.
E. To keep Banquo from learning the truth about Duncan's murder.

_____3.   Why does Macbeth's plot against Banquo fail?

A. Donalbain escapes.
B. Fleance escapes.
C. Malcolm escapes.
D. Banquo escapes.
E. Ross escapes.

_____4. Why does Lady Macbeth make excuses for Macbeth's reactions to seeing Banquo's ghost?

  A. She also sees the ghost but wishes to appear brave.
  B. She knows that her husband is insane.
  C. She wishes to maintain the appearance that Macbeth is still in control.
  D. She wants her guests to enjoy themselves.
  E. She wants Macbeth to appear foolish, so that she can assume power.

_____5. How does Macbeth interpret the appearance of Banquo's ghost?

  A. That the murder of Duncan will be avenged.
  B. That his plot against Banquo has failed.
  C. That his plot against Banquo has succeeded.
  D. That the witches are up to no good.
  E. That Malcolm is returning to Scotland.

NAME:_____   DATE: _____

Postreading Activity
for
Macbeth
Small Group Discussion to Check Comprehension
Act III

Directions: After you've read all of Act III, discuss each of the following questions in small groups briefly. Use the space below each question to note points you may want to share later. If you need more room, use the back of the page.

1. What has Macbeth done in his previous meeting with the murderers to convince them to kill Banquo?

2. What has Macbeth to gain from having Banquo murdered?

3. What causes Macbeth's plot against Banquo to fail ultimately?

4. What does Lady Macbeth do when Macbeth sees the ghost of Banquo?

5. How does Macbeth interpret the appearance of Banquo's ghost?

NAME:_____   DATE: _____

Postreading Activity
for
Macbeth
Critical Thinking Questions
Act III

Directions: To help you develop your understanding of Act III, as your teacher directs you, take time to think about and discuss the following questions. The first question is the focus question and is the point of the discussion. Don't be concerned that you may not be able to answer this question at first. Proceed to the exploration questions and then return to the focus question.

Focus Question. To what extent do you think Macbeth's corruption is due to weaknesses within his character and to what extent do you think his corruption is due to external forces?

Exploration Questions.

1. When do you feel it is appropriate to seize control of a situation?

2. In this act we see Macbeth and Lady Macbeth as king and queen for the first time. How have they changed as a result of their new positions?

3. Give examples of leaders whom you feel have abused their power, and briefly state the reasons for your choices.

4. When would you feel it would be necessary to overthrow an existing government?

5. Now that Macbeth has seized the throne, what suggests that he may not be secure in his power?

6. Compare Macbeth's position with that of a current leader whom you consider corrupt.

NAME:_____   DATE: _____

Postreading Activity
for
Macbeth
Language Exploration
Symbol
Act III

When we use a word, object, or image to represent another idea or concept, it becomes a *symbol*. For example, the American flag is a symbol of our country and its democratic form of government. Another example would be when people drive luxury automobiles or wear expensive watches as symbols to show that they have enough wealth to afford these items.

In literature, too, authors often use symbols. For example, in Act I, scene ii, note the animals that the captain uses before he describes how Macbeth and Banquo responded to the Norwegians' counter attack:

❧

DUNCAN
Dismayed not this
Our captains, Macbeth and Banquo?

CAPTAIN
As sparrows eagles, or the hare the lion.

❧

Here Macbeth and Banquo are compared to eagles and lions—symbols of power, courage, and nobility—while the Norwegians are compared to sparrows and hares—timid or weak animals.

Directions: The following lines contain symbols. Working in pairs, small groups, or as your teacher directs, review each passage in the context of the play and decide what each symbol suggests to the reader.

1.   Ross speaking of Macbeth's bravery in battle (Act I, scene ii):

❧

. . . Norway himself,
With terrible numbers,
Assisted by that most disloyal traitor,
The Thane of Cawdor, began a dismal conflict,
Till that Bellona's bridegroom, lapped in proof,

125

Confronted him with self-comparisons,
Point against point, rebellious arm 'gainst arm,
Curbing his lavish spirit; and to conclude,
The victory fell on us.

అ

2.   The witch explaining how she'll take revenge upon the sailor's wife by
       going to the sailor's ship (Act I, scene iii):

అ

But in a sieve I'll thither sail,
And like a rat without a tail,
I'll do, I'll do, I'll do.

అ

3.   Macbeth's response to his new title (Act I, scene iii):

అ

The Thane of Cawdor lives. Why do you dress me
In borrowed robes?

అ

4.   Lady Macbeth rousing her courage (Act I, scene v):

అ

. . . Come to my woman's breasts,
And take milk for gall, you murd'ring ministers,
Wherever in your sightless substances
You wait on nature's mischief.

అ

© 1994 by The Center for Applied Research in Education

5. Macbeth responding to Lady Macbeth's plan to make sure the guards sleep through the murder (Act I, scene vii):

    ❧

    Bring forth men-children only
    For thy undaunted mettle should compose
    Nothing but males.

    ❧

6. Macbeth addressing the vision of the dagger (Act II, scene i);

    ❧

    Is this a dagger which I see before me,
    The handle toward my hand? Come let me clutch thee.
    I have thee not, and yet I see thee still.
    Art thou not, fatal vision, sensible
    To feeling as to sight?

    ❧

7. Macbeth responding to murdering the King (Act II, scene iii):

    ❧

    Will all great Neptune's oceans wash this blood
    Clean from my hand? No. This my hand will rather
    The multitudinous seas incarnadine,
    Making the green one red.

    ❧

127

8.   Macbeth describing the dead body of Duncan (Act II, scene iii):

 za

> *. . . Here lay Duncan,*
> *His silver skin laced with his golden blood,*

za

9.   Ross describing the strange events of the day (Act II, scene iv):

za

> *And Duncan's horses—a thing most strange and certain—*
> *Beauteous, and swift, the minions of their race,*
> *Turned wild in nature, broke their stalls, flung out,*
> *Contending 'gainst obedience, as they would*
> *Make war with mankind.*

za

10. Macbeth commenting on his seizure of power and possible opposition
     to it (Act III, scene ii):

za

> *We have scotched the snake, not killed it.*
> *She'll close, and be herself, whilst our poor malice*
> *Remains in danger of her former tooth.*

za

© 1994 by The Center for Applied Research in Education

Postreading Activity
for
Macbeth
Vocabulary in Context
Act III

Directions: In each of the passages below you will find one of the words from the prereading vocabulary list for Act III. Review the definitions given in the prereading vocabulary. Working individually, in pairs, or in small groups as your teacher directs, examine each of the underlined words in the following passages from Act III. For each word, use the appropriate meaning and develop a brief interpretation of the passage within the context of the play.

1. Banquo commenting upon the witches' prophecies for Macbeth and him (scene i):

&

> . . . *If there come truth from them,*
> *As upon thee Macbeth, their speeches shine,*
> *Why by the <u>verities</u> on thee made good*
> *May not be my oracles as well,*
> *And set me up in hope?*

&

2. Banquo replying to King Macbeth's invitation to attend the banquet (scene i):

&

> *Let you Highness*
> *Command upon me, to the which my duties*
> *Are the most <u>indissoluble</u> tie*
> *For ever knit.*

&

3. Macbeth commenting upon the whereabouts of Malcolm and Donalbain (scene i):

🍂

We hear our bloody cousins are bestowed
In England and in Ireland, not confessing
Their cruel parricide, filling the hearers
With strange <u>invention</u>.

🍂

4. Macbeth commenting upon the witches' prophecy that Banquo's descendants should be kings (scene i):

🍂

Upon my head they placed a fruitless crown,
And put a barren sceptre in my gripe,
Thence to be wrenched with an <u>unlineal</u> hand,
No son of mine succeeding.

🍂

5. Macbeth recounting how Banquo had wronged the murderers (scene i):

🍂

. . .This I made good to you
In our last conference; passed in <u>probation</u> with you
How you were borne in hand, how crossed; the instruments,
Who wrought with them; and all things else that might
To half a soul, and to a notion crazed,
Say, thus did Banquo.

🍂

© 1994 by The Center for Applied Research in Education

6.   Lady Macbeth to Macbeth (scene ii):

ào

How now my lord, why do you keep alone,
Of sorriest <u>fancies</u> your companions making,
Using those thoughts which should indeed have died
With them they think on?

ào

7.   Macbeth to Lady Macbeth (scene ii):

ào

We have <u>scotched</u> the snake, not killed it.

ào

8.   Lady Macbeth advising her husband to be the jovial host (scene ii):

ào

Gentle my lord, <u>sleek</u> o'er your rugged looks,
Be bright and jovial among your guests tonight.

ào

9.   Macbeth commenting on his plans to hide the murder of Banquo and Fleance from his wife (scene ii):

ào

Be innocent of the knowledge, dearest chuck,
Till thou applaud the deed. Come <u>seeling</u> night,
Scarf up the tender eye of pitiful day,

ào

131

10. Lady Macbeth urging her husband to be more the jovial host (scene iv):

&

My royal lord,
You do not give the cheer. The feast is sold
That is not often <u>vouched</u>, while 'tis a-making,
'Tis given with welcome.

&

Vocabulary Review Quiz
for
Macbeth
Act III

Directions: For each of the italicized words in the sentences below, determine which letter best reflects the use of the word in this context. Place the letter corresponding to your answer in the space to the left of the item number.

_____1. Banquo comments upon the witches' prophecies, calling them *verities*; this suggests that
A. he believes the witches to be mortal
B. he distrusts the witches
C. he understands who the witches really are
D. he accepts the truth of the prophecies
E. he suspects that the prophecies are only true for a short while

_____2. When Banquo suggests that his ties to King Macbeth are *indissoluble*, he means that
A. they are vows broken easily
B. they are binding obligations
C. they are only words
D. they are knotty problems
E. they are plots to kill him

_____3. Saying that Malcolm and Donalbain fill their hearers with *invention*, Macbeth suggests
A. they are telling lies
B. they are planning to kill him
C. they are writing novels
D. they are making new war machines
E. they are paranoid

_____4. Macbeth is troubled by the visions of the *unlineal* kings because it means
A. the kings will be unruly
B. the kings will be tyrants
C. Macbeth will have no descendants
D. collateral descendants of Duncan
E. Macbeth's son will be king after Malcolm

_____5. When Macbeth mentions to the murderers that he discussed their wrongs in *probation*, he means
A. he asked their pardon for hurting them.
B. he asked to be remembered in their prayers.
C. he proved it was Banquo who wronged them.
D. he defended Banquo to them.
E. he forgave them their insults.

_____6. When Lady Macbeth tells her husband not to worry about *fancies*, she means
A. plans that have been discovered.
B. her infidelities.
C. someone is out to damage his reputation.
D. ideas with little foundation.
E. elaborate plots against him.

_____7. As Macbeth uses *scotch* he means
A. liquor.
B. burn lightly.
C. scrape.
D. render harmless temporarily.
E. kill.

_____8. To *sleek* means to
A. roughen up.
B. smooth over.
C. look at intensely.
D. refuse.
E. surrender.

_____9. Macbeth describes night as *seeling*; he means it
A. hovers above people.
B. can cement people together.
C. can blind people.
D. sees evil.
E. protects Duncan.

_____10. *Vouch* means to
A. defend.
B. guarantee.
C. leave.
D. threaten.
E. deny.

ACT IV

Focusing Activities
for
Macbeth
Scenarios for Improvisation
Act IV

Directions: Presented below are locations and situations involving characters. As your teacher directs you, but before reading an individual scene, pretend to be one of the characters and act out the situation. Don't worry about speaking like the characters in Shakespeare's plays, just try to imagine how you would react to the situation and use your own language. Your teacher may give you a few minutes to discuss what you would like to do with the other performers. Your teacher will probably ask you to act out your scene for others in the class. When you finish, your teacher may ask your classmates to discuss what they've seen.

scene i.   *Scene:* Witches' cavern.

Characters: The three witches and Macbeth.

Situation: Macbeth has come to the witches to find out the worst from them. In light of Hecate's speech to the witches in Act III, scene v, improvise the scene between them.

scene iii.   *Scene:* Malcolm's quarters at King Edward's castle in England.

Characters: Malcolm and Macduff.

Situation: Macduff arrives and informs Malcolm of the tyrant that Macbeth has become and urges Malcolm to join with English forces and oppose Macbeth. Improvise the scene between them.

137

NAME:_____   DATE:_____

Focusing Activities
for
Macbeth
Small Group Discussion Questions
Act IV

Directions: Before reading the scenes in Act IV, discuss the following questions in small groups. You may wish to make notes about your discussion, so you can share it with classmates or refer back to it after you've read the scene.

scene i. In Act III, scene iv, Macbeth promised to go to the witches again "for now I am bent to know/ By the worst means the worst, for mine own good." In light of Hecate's speech to the witches in Act III, scene v, what do you think they will tell him?

scene ii. At the end of scene i, Macbeth vows vengeance upon Macduff. What do you think Macbeth has to gain by murdering Macduff's wife and children? What does he have to lose?

scene iii. If you were Macduff meeting with Malcolm in England, what might you ask Malcolm to do? As Malcolm, how might you respond to Macduff's request?

NAME:_____   DATE:_____

Focusing Activities
for
Macbeth
Speculation Journal
Act IV

Directions: This activity is to help you become involved actively with reading the play by helping you to determine a definite purpose for reading. Before you read these scenes in Act IV, take a few minutes to respond in writing to the questions below. Don't worry about correct answers here. Use your own experience, what you know, or what you may have heard about the play to speculate about what you think might happen. After reading a scene, you may find that the characters reacted differently than you thought. Don't worry about these differences; just make note of them because you will have opportunities to share these differences in other activities.

scene i. In Act III, scene iv, Macbeth vowed to go to the witches again "for now I am bent to know/ By the worst means the worst, for mine own good." What do you think they will tell him?

scene ii. Based upon what Macbeth has learned from the witches and his sworn vengeance upon Macduff, what do you think he will do to Macduff's family?

scene iii. When Macduff meets with Malcolm in England, what do you think he will ask Malcolm to do?

After reading Act IV: Now that you have finished reading Act IV, which of your speculations were most accurate? How do you account for them? Which ones were least like the action of the play? Why do you think you speculated as you did?

139

Prereading Activity for
Macbeth
Vocabulary
Act IV

Directions: Shakespeare uses the following words in Act IV. The section below provides a brief definition of each word and provides a sentence to illustrate its meaning. You may want to review the words for a particular scene immediately before reading it.

Definitions

scene i

1. **harp:** (v.) to give voice or utterance to.
   Example: In the eulogy, the minister *harped* many of the emotions of the entire congregation attending the funeral.

2. **potent:** (adj.) powerful; influential.
   Example: Some varieties of chili peppers are more *potent* than others.

3. **impress:** (v.) conscript, draft, force into military or other service.
   Example: In Shakespeare's time, gangs of sailors often kidnapped unsuspecting young men and *impressed* them into service aboard ship.

4. **perni-cious:** (adj.) harmful; destructive; lethal.
   Example: The *pernicious* fumes of ammonia spread across the city.

5. **firstling:** (n.) the first of a kind; first-born offspring.
   Example: Macbeth's murdering of Duncan was a *firstling* of evil.

scene ii

6. **school:** (v.) to inform, teach, train.
   Example: We have failed to *school* our miniature schnauzer not to bark every time someone knocks on the front door.

scene iii

7. **desolate:** (adj.) isolated; lonely.
   Example: Until the small boy made friends at camp, he felt it was a *desolate* place that his parents had sent him to.

8. **intemp-** (n.) excessive indulgence of a natural appetite or passion; **erance:** lack of moderation.
   Example: Andy's *intemperance* about driving fast has resulted in several speeding tickets.

9. **avarice:** (n.) insatiable greed for riches; inordinate desire to gain or hoard wealth.
   Example: King Midas' *avarice* was ultimately the cause of his own downfall.

10. **scruples:** (n.) tiny parts; doubt; difficulty.
    Example: Our young son has no *scruples* in accepting anyone's friendship, so he often gets used by others.

Prereading Activity
for
Macbeth
Plot Summaries
Act IV

Directions: To help you better understand and follow *Macbeth,* read the summary of a specific scene before you begin to read it. If you get lost during the scene, you can refer to the summary.

Act IV, scene i

As the witches brew a potion in a cauldron, Macbeth enters. He demands that the witches answer his questions even though it may unleash destruction on the land. The witches agree to answer. Three apparitions rise from the cauldron and speak to Macbeth. The first, an armed head, warns him of Macduff, the Thane of Fife. The second apparition, a bloody child, promises that no man born of woman shall harm Macbeth. Macbeth's response to the second apparition is that because Macduff was born of a woman, he cannot harm him. The third apparition, a child wearing a crown and carrying a tree in its hand, promises that Macbeth shall not be defeated until Birnam Wood marches on Dunsinane Hill. Macbeth's response is that it is impossible for trees to uproot themselves and move on their own, so he must be safe. He then asks whether Banquo's descendants will ever reign over Scotland. The witches show him a string of eight kings, the last with a glass in his hand. The witches then vanish.

Act IV, scene ii

At Fife, Macduff's castle, Lady Macduff and her son learn from Ross that her husband has departed for England. She presumes that her husband has fled to save his own life rather than gone to seek the assistance of the English against Macbeth. Ross leaves to join Macduff in England.

When they are alone, Lady Macduff supposes that Macduff is dead, but her son refuses to believe so. A messenger comes to warn Lady Macduff of approaching danger, but she protests that she is innocent. Macbeth's assassins enter and slaughter all the children and Lady Macduff.

© 1994 by The Center for Applied Research in Education

Act IV,
scene iii
In England, Macduff meets with Malcolm. Macduff tells Malcolm of Macbeth's constant tyranny and murder. Malcolm points out that Macbeth may not have harmed him yet, but he should be wary.

The war to restore Malcolm must not be contaminated by the evil of Macbeth's reign. Macduff wants action, but Malcolm seems to want to wait, so that he can test Macduff's loyalty.

Ross enters and tells them that Macbeth's murderous reign has continued, making Macduff fear for the safety of his family. Ross reluctantly tells him that Macbeth has had them all murdered. Macduff vows to avenge the deaths.

Class Period:

CHARACTER ASSIGNMENTS FOR ORAL READING GROUPS

Macbeth

Session 6: Act IV, scenes i, ii, iii

Characters	*Group 1*	*Group 2*	*Group 3*	*Group 4*
First Witch, Lady Macduff	_____	_____	_____	_____
Second Witch, Malcolm	_____	_____	_____	_____
Third Witch, Messenger	_____	_____	_____	_____
Hecate, English Doctor	_____	_____	_____	_____
Macbeth	_____	_____	_____	_____
First Apparition, Ross, First Murderer	_____	_____	_____	_____
Second Apparition, Macduff's son	_____	_____	_____	_____
Third Apparition, Macduff	_____	_____	_____	_____

144

NAME:_____   DATE:_____

During-reading Activity
for
Macbeth
Character Diary 6
Act IV, scenes i, ii, iii

Directions: Use the space below to record your character's reactions to the events of the three scenes in Act IV of *Macbeth*. Remember to include a summary of events, explain how your character learned of them, and give your character's reactions to them. Because this act has three scenes, you may want to record your character's entries as you read each scene. If you need additional room, use the back of this sheet.

The Personal Diary of

_____
(character's name)

Scenes i and ii
The next day

_____

_____

_____

_____

_____

_____

_____

Scene iii
A week or so later

_____

_____

_____

_____

_____

_____

**During-reading Activity
for
Macbeth
Viewing Act IV, scene i
Macbeth Returns to the Witches

Directions: After you've read this scene, viewing a film or video version may help you better understand how the text translates into the characters' actions. Although you may want to keep your copy of the play handy, don't be surprised if the actors' script varies from yours. Film scripts often delete or reorder the lines in the play. You may want to note questions you need to ask your teacher afterwards. After viewing the scene, take a few minutes to respond to the questions below.

1.   Based upon what you've seen, how do the witches react to Macbeth's demands to know the future?

2.   How does Macbeth react to each of the prophecies?

3.   Why do you think the director has chosen to present the apparitions in the manner they are in this production?

NAME:_____   DATE:_____

During-reading Activity
for
Macbeth
Guide to Character Development: Macbeth
Act IV

Shakespeare reveals his characters in four ways:

ɞ through what the characters say to other characters in dialogue;

ɞ through what the characters reveal about their thoughts through long speeches to the audience called *soliloquies;*

ɞ through what other characters say about them;

ɞ through what they do, their actions.

As you read the play, examine the following scenes for what they reveal about Macbeth's character and fill in the chart briefly using your own words. If you need more room, use the back of the page.

Scene	What Macbeth says, does, or what others say about him	What this reveals about Macbeth's character
Act IV, scene i Macbeth meets the witches a second time		
Act IV, scene i Lennox informs Macbeth that Macduff has fled to England		
Act IV, scene iii Macbeth has Macduff's family murdered		

During-reading Activity
for
Macbeth
Guide to Character Development: Macduff
Act IV

Shakespeare reveals his characters in four ways:

ᎧᎦ through what the characters say to other characters in dialogue;

ᎧᎦ through what the characters reveal about their thoughts through long speeches to the audience called *soliloquies;*

ᎧᎦ through what other characters say about them;

ᎧᎦ through what they do, their actions.

As you read the play, examine the following scenes for what they reveal about Macduff's character and fill in the chart briefly using your own words. If you need more room, use the back of the page.

Scene	What Macduff says, does, or what others say about him	What this reveals about Macduff's character
Act IV, scene ii Macduff flees to England		
Act IV, scene iii Macduff meets with Malcolm		
Act IV, scene iii Ross tells Macduff that Macbeth has murdered his wife and children		

NAME:_____   DATE:_____

During-reading Activity
for
Macbeth
Guide to Character Development: Ross
Act IV

Shakespeare reveals his characters in four ways:

- through what the characters say to other characters in dialogue;
- through what the characters reveal about their thoughts through long speeches to the audience called *soliloquies;*
- through what other characters say about them;
- through what they do, their actions.

As you read the play, examine the following scenes for what they reveal about Ross's character and fill in the chart briefly using your own words. If you need more room, use the back of the page.

Scene	What Ross says, does, or what others say about him	What this reveals about Ross's character
Act IV, scene ii Macduff goes to England		
Act IV, scene ii Ross goes to England		
Act IV, scene iii Ross tells Macduff that Macbeth has murdered his wife and children		

During-reading Activity
for
Macbeth
Guide to Character Development: Malcolm
Act IV

Shakespeare reveals his characters in four ways:

- through what the characters say to other characters in dialogue;
- through what the characters reveal about their thoughts through long speeches to the audience called *soliloquies;*
- through what other characters say about them;
- through what they do, their actions.

As you read the play, examine the following scene for what it reveals about Malcolm's character and fill in the chart briefly using your own words. If you need more room, use the back of the page.

Scene	What Malcolm does, says, or what others say about him	What this reveals about Malcolm's character
Act IV, iii Malcolm meets with Macduff		

© 1994 by The Center for Applied Research in Education

NAME:_____ DATE:_____

During-reading Activity
for
Macbeth
Guide to Character Development: The Witches
Act IV

Shakespeare reveals his characters in four ways:

- through what the characters say to other characters in dialogue;
- through what the characters reveal about their thoughts through long speeches to the audience called *soliloquies;*
- through what other characters say about them;
- through what they do, their actions.

As you read the play, examine the following scene for what it reveals about the witches' characters and fill in the chart briefly using your own words. If you need more room, use the back of the page.

Scene	What the witches say, do, or what others say about them	What this reveals about the witches' characters
Act IV, i The witches meet with Macbeth		

Postreading Activity
for
Macbeth
Comprehension Check
Act IV

Directions: After you've read all of Act IV, use the following questions to check how well you've understood what you've read. For each question, select the most appropriate answer from the choices listed below it. Place the letter corresponding to your answer in the space to the left of the item number.

_____1.   Why does Macbeth believe he has nothing to fear from Macduff?

    A. Because Macbeth is stronger.
    B. Because Macduff has sworn to be loyal to Macbeth.
    C. Because Macbeth is immortal.
    D. Because "none of woman born shall harm Macbeth."
    E. Because Macduff has fled to England.

_____2.   What do the witches show Macbeth that confirms the failure of his plot against Banquo?

    A. A vision of an armed head.
    B. A vision of a bloody child.
    C. A vision of a line of kings.
    D. A vision of trees with weapons.
    E. A vision of a child wearing a crown.

_____3.   Why does Macbeth fear the last vision that the witches show him?

    A. Because he knows that he's a lost soul.
    B. Because he realizes that he will have no heir.
    C. Because it shows the death of Lady Macbeth.
    D. Because he realizes the witches are agents of evil.
    E. Because it shows Malcolm returning to power.

    ____4.   Why does Macbeth order the slaughter of Macduff's wife and children?

        A. To punish Macduff for refusing to attend the banquet.

        B. To avenge the murder of Duncan.

        C. To scare Macduff into exile.

        D. To punish Macduff for joining forces with Malcolm.

        E. To provoke Macduff into battle.

    ____5.   Why does Malcolm hesitate to join Macduff in overthrowing Macbeth?

        A. To test Macduff's loyalty.

        B. To avoid a battle with Macbeth.

        C. To wait until he has reinforcements from Donalbain.

        D. To take revenge for his father's death.

        E. To learn what Macbeth's battle plan is.

Postreading Activity
for
Macbeth
Small Group Discussion to Check Comprehension
Act IV

Directions: After you've read all of Act IV, discuss each of the following questions in small groups briefly. Use the space below each question to note points you may want to share later. If you need more room, use the back of the page.

1. Why does Macbeth go to see the witches a second time?

2. How does Macbeth interpret the first three visions that the witches show him?

3. Why does Macbeth become upset when he sees the fourth vision?

4. What does Macbeth's ordering of the slaughter of Macduff's family show us about Macbeth's character at this point in the play?

5. What does Malcolm gain by not committing to join Macduff against Macbeth when Macduff first asks?

Postreading Activity
for
Macbeth
Critical Thinking Questions
Act IV

Directions: To help you develop your understanding of Act IV, as your teacher directs you, take time to think about and discuss the following questions. The first question is the focus question and is the point of the discussion. Don't be concerned that you may not be able to answer this question at first. Proceed to the exploration questions and then return to the focus question.

Focus Question. Based upon the play, what would lead you to believe that Macbeth would or wouldn't be convicted for his crimes in a modern court?

Exploration Questions.

1. From your experience, what motivates a person to act desperately?

2. What occurs during the act that suggests Macbeth's power is waning?

3. Compare and contrast Macbeth's ruthlessness to that of another character in literature you're familiar with.

4. How do you determine whether a literary character is good or evil?

5. What has Macbeth done that suggests to you he's become evil?

6. As compared to some of the violent criminals around today, to what extent is Macbeth better or worse than they?

Postreading Activity
for
Macbeth
Language Exploration.
Imagery
Act IV

In addition to figurative language, symbolism, and verbal irony, Shakespeare also uses *imagery:* language that appeals to the senses of *sight, touch, taste, smell,* and *hearing*. Because our senses provide our direct contact with the world, poets often appeal to these concrete experiences to help convey more abstract ideas. Shakespeare often develops imagery in combination with figurative language.

Notice how Lady Macbeth appeals to the senses and reveals her desire to have the resolve to murder Duncan (Act I, scene v):

The raven himself is hoarse
That croaks the fatal entrance of Duncan   *(sound)*
Under my battlements. Come you spirits
That tend on mortal thoughts, unsex me here,
And fill me from the crown to the toe top-full
Of direst cruelty; make thick my blood,   *(sight)*
Stop up th' access and passage to remorse,
That no compunctious visitings of nature
Shake my fell purpose, nor keep peace between
Th' effect and it. Come to my woman's breasts,
And take my milk for gall, you murd'ring ministers,   *(taste)*
Wherever in your sightless substances
You wait on nature's mischief. Come thick night,   *(sight)*
And pall thee in the dunnest smoke of hell,   *(smell)*
That my keen knife see not the wound it makes,   *(sight)*
Nor heaven peep through the blanket of the dark,   *(sight)*
To cry, hold, hold!   *(hearing)*

Directions: The following passages from Acts III and IV contain examples of imagery. Working in pairs, small groups, or as your teacher directs, review each passage in the context of the play and decide which sense Shakespeare appeals to and what the passage suggests to the reader.

© 1994 by The Center for Applied Research in Education

1. Banquo reflecting upon the truth of the witches' prophecies (Act III, scene i):

    ❧

    > . . . . *If there come truth from them,*
    > *As upon thee Macbeth, their speeches shine,*
    > *Why by the verities on thee made good*
    > *May they not be my oracles as well,*
    > *And set me up in hope?*

    ❧

2. Macbeth reflecting upon possible threats to his power (Act III, scene ii):

    ❧

    > *We have scotched the snake, not killed it.*
    > *She'll close, and be herself, whilst our poor malice*
    > *Remains in danger of her former tooth.*

    ❧

3. Macbeth referring to his plans to have Banquo murdered (Act III, scene ii):

    ❧

    > *Be innocent of the knowledge, dearest chuck,*
    > *Till thou applaud the deed. Come seeling night,*
    > *Scarf up the tender eye of pitiful day,*
    > *And with thy bloody and invisible hand*
    > *Cancel and tear to pieces that great bond*
    > *Which keeps me pale.*

    ❧

4. The First Murderer before killing Banquo (Act III, scene iii):

The west yet glimmers with some streaks of day.

5. Lady Macbeth urging Macbeth to be a jovial host (Act III, scene iv):

My royal lord,
You do not give the cheer. The feast is sold
That is not often vouched, while 'tis a-making,
'Tis given with welcome. To feed were best at home;
From thence, the sauce to meat is ceremony,
Meeting were bare without it.

6. Macbeth addressing Banquo's ghost (Act III, scene iv):

Avaunt, and quit my sight, let the earth hide thee!
Thy bones are marrowless, thy blood is cold.
Thou has no speculation in those eyes
Which thou dost glare with.

7. Macbeth has disrupted the banquet with his ranting at Banquo's ghost (Act III, scene iv):

It will have blood, they say; blood will have blood.
Stones have been known to move, and trees to speak.

8. Macduff describing Macbeth's tyranny to Malcolm (Act IV, scene iii):

Let us rather
Hold fast the mortal sword; and like good men,
Bestride our down-fallen birthdom. Each new morn,
New widows howl, new orphans cry, new sorrows
Strike heaven on the face, that it resounds
As if it felt with Scotland, and yelled out
Like syllable of dolor.

9. Malcolm commenting on his fear that he may be more of a tyrant than Macbeth (Act IV, scene iii):

It is myself I mean; in whom I know
All the particulars of vice so grafted,
That when they shall be opened, black Macbeth
Will seem as pure as snow, and the poor state
Esteem him as a lamb, being compared
With my confineless harms.

10. Malcolm resolved to attack Macbeth once Macduff vows revenge (Act IV, scene iii):

ɞ

This tune goes manly.
Come go we to the King, our power is ready,
Our lack is nothing but our leave. Macbeth
Is ripe for shaking, and the powers above
Put on their instruments. Receive what cheer you may
The night is long that never finds the day.

ɞ

NAME:_____   DATE:_____

Postreading Activity
for
Macbeth
Vocabulary in Context
Act IV

Directions: In each of the passages below you will find one of the words from the prereading vocabulary list for Act IV. Review the definitions given in the prereading vocabulary. Working individually, in pairs, or in small groups as your teacher directs, examine each of the underlined words in the following passages from Act IV. For each word, use the appropriate meaning and develop a brief interpretation of the passage within the context of the play.

1. Macbeth commenting on the warning of the first apparition (scene i):

~

Whate'er thou art, for thy good caution thanks,
Thou hast <u>harped</u> my fear aright. But one word more—

~

2. First witch pointing out the appearance of the second apparition (scene i):

~

. . . .Here's another,
More <u>potent</u> than the first.

~

161

3.   Macbeth commenting on the third apparition's warning (scene i):

&

That will never be.
Who can <u>impress</u> the forest, bid the tree
Unfix his earth-bound root?

&

4.   Macbeth responding to the vision of the line of kings descended from Banquo (scene i):

&

Where are they? Gone? Let this <u>pernicious</u> hour
Stand aye accursed in the calendar.

&

5.   Macbeth vowing vengeance on Macduff (scene i):

&

. . . .From this moment
The very <u>firstlings</u> of my heart shall be
The <u>firstlings</u> of my hand.

&

6.   Ross trying to warn Lady Macduff (scene ii):

ઢ

My dearest coz,
I pray you __school__ yourself.

ઢ

7.   Malcolm to Macduff (scene iii):

ઢ

Let us seek out some __desolate__ shade, and there
Weep our sad bosoms empty.

ઢ

8.   Macduff commenting on Macbeth's tyranny (scene iii):

ઢ

Boundless __intemperance__
In nature is a tyranny; it hath been
Th' untimely emptying of the happy throne,
And fall of many kings.

ઢ

9.   Malcolm commenting on how he might react to growing power (scene iii):

ಬಿ

With this, there grows
In my most ill-composed affection, such
A stauchless avarice, that were I King,
I should cut off the nobles for their lands,
Desire his jewels, and this other's houses,
And my more-having would be a sauce
To make me hunger more, that I should forge
Quarrels unjust against the good and loyal,
Destroying them for wealth.

ಬಿ

10.   Malcolm addressing Macduff (scene iii):

ಬಿ

Macduff, this noble passion,
Child of integrity, hath from my soul
Wiped the black scruples, reconciled my thoughts
To thy good truth and honor.

ಬಿ

© 1994 by The Center for Applied Research in Education

Vocabulary Review Quiz
for
Macbeth
Act IV

Directions: For each of the italicized words in the sentences below, determine which letter best reflects the use of the word in its context. Place the letter corresponding to your answer in the space to the left of the item number.

_____1.   When Macbeth says that the first apparition *harped* his fear, he means it

A. eased his fear   B. voiced his fear   C. has increased his fear
D. sung away his fear   E. made Macbeth more bold

_____2.   *Potent* means
A. powerful   B. virile   C. courageous   D. cowardly   E. angry

_____3.   When Macbeth feels safe because no one can *impress* a forest, he means no one can

A. cut down his trees   B. do more than tend trees
C. make a good impression on trees   D. draft the trees
E. march like trees

_____4.   *Pernicious* means
A. angry   B. divisive   C. destructive   D. determined   E. dastardly

_____5.   Macbeth swears to take his revenge on Macduff's *firstlings;* therefore, Macbeth plans to attack Macduff's
A. castle   B. heirs   C. armies   D. concerns   E. lands

_____6.   When Ross urges Lady Macduff to *school* herself, he means she needs to

A. request pardon of Macbeth   B. train herself as a soldier
C. raise an army to protect herself   D. learn to be more courteous
E. inform herself of reality

_____7.   When Malcolm suggests he and Macduff seek out some *desolate* shade, he means

A. a barren wilderness   B. a crowded room   C. an empty room
D. a dead tree   E. an isolated place

© 1994 by The Center for Applied Research in Education

_____8. When Malcolm suggests Macbeth shows *intemperance,* he means Macbeth is

A. excessively indulgent   B. excessively angry   C. unduly interested
D. only moderately powerful   E. losing his mind

_____9. Macbeth is guilty of *avarice;* therefore, he is

A. insatiably hungry for food and drink   B. insatiably greedy for wealth
C. insatiably angry with his nobles   D. undeniably insane
E. unstoppable

_____10. During the scene with Malcolm, Macduff relieves the Prince of any *scruples* he has about Macduff; therefore, Malcolm

A. has no doubts about Macduff's loyalty   B. still cannot trust Macduff
completely   C. needs to test Macduff's loyalty further   D. doesn't trust
Macduff's judgment   E. comes to understand Macduff's motives

ACT V

© 1994 by The Center for Applied Research in Education

NAME:_____   DATE:_____

Focusing Activities
for
Macbeth
Scenarios for Improvisation
Act V

Directions: Presented below are locations and situations involving characters. As your teacher directs you, but before reading an individual scene, pretend to be one of the characters and act out the situation. Don't worry about speaking like the characters in Shakespeare's plays, just try to imagine how you would react to the situation and use your own language. Your teacher may give you a few minutes to discuss what you would like to do with the other performers. Your teacher will probably ask you to act out your scene for others in the class. When you finish, your teacher may ask your classmates to discuss what they've seen.

scene i. Scene: The royal palace, late at night.

Characters: A doctor, a gentlewoman who attends Lady Macbeth.

Situation: The gentlewoman has seen Lady Macbeth sleepwalk and act very strangely for several nights. She's contacted the doctor to come and observe. Improvise Lady Macbeth's sleepwalking and what she might say or recall while asleep and the reactions of her unknown audience to it.

scene viii. Scene: The royal palace.

Characters: Macbeth and Macduff.

Situation: Malcolm's forces have overrun the castle. Macduff and Macbeth meet. Before they engage in combat, improvise the dialogue between them.

Focusing Activities
for
Macbeth
Small Group Discussion Questions
Act V

Directions: Before reading the scenes in Act V, discuss the following questions in small groups. You may want to make notes about your discussion so you can share them with classmates or refer back to them after you've read each scene.

scene i. Now that Malcolm and Macduff are supported with English troops and have decided to depose Macbeth, how do you think the impeding war and prospect of defeat might affect Lady Macbeth?

scene ii. If you were a playwright, how might you show that additional nobles supported Malcolm and Macduff's war against Macbeth?

scene iii. How do you think Macbeth might respond to the Doctor's diagnosis that Lady Macbeth is mentally rather than physically ill?

scene iv.   How might Malcolm make it seem that the forest is attacking the castle?

scene v.   How do you think Macbeth will respond when he learns that the forest is approaching the castle?

scenes vi, vii, viii.   Malcolm made the prophecy about Birnam Wood coming to Dunsinane come true. What "loopholes" might there be in the remaining prophecies that would allow them to come true as well?

Focusing Activities
for
Macbeth
Speculation Journal
Act V

Directions: This activity is to help you become involved actively with reading the play by helping you to determine a definite purpose for reading. Before you read these scenes in Act V, take a few minutes to respond in writing to the questions below. Don't worry about correct answers here. Use your own experience, what you know, or what you may have heard about the play to speculate about what you think might happen. After reading a scene, you may find that the characters reacted differently than you thought. Don't worry about these differences; just make note of them because you will have opportunities to share these differences in other activities.

scene i. Now that Malcolm and Macduff are supported with English troops and have decided to depose Macbeth, how do you think the impeding war and possible defeat might affect Lady Macbeth?

scene ii. If you were a playwright, how might you show that additional nobles supported Malcolm and Macduff's war against Macbeth?

scene iii. How do you think Macbeth might respond to the Doctor's diagnosis that Lady Macbeth is mentally rather than physically ill?

scene iv. How might Malcolm make it seem that the forest is attacking the castle?

© 1994 by The Center for Applied Research in Education

scene v.   How do you think Macbeth will respond when he learns that the forest is approaching the castle?

scenes   Malcolm made the prophecy about Birnam Wood coming to Dunsinane
vi, vii, viii.   come true. What "loopholes" might there be in the remaining prophecies that would allow them to come true as well?

After   Now that you have finished reading Act V, which of your speculations
reading   were most accurate? How do you account for them? Which ones were
Act V: least like the action of the play? Why do you think you speculated as you did?

Prereading Activity
for
Macbeth
Vocabulary
Act V

Directions: Shakespeare uses the following words in Act V. The section below provides a brief definition of each word and provides a sentence to illustrate its meaning. You may want to review the words for a particular scene immediately before reading it.

Definitions.

scene i

1. **perturbation:** (n.) a mental agitation.
   Example: Embezzling funds from the charity became such a *perturbation* that the director turned herself in to the police.

2. **charge:** (v.) to suffuse with emotion.
   Example: *Charged* with sorrow, the final scene of the movie caused many viewers to leave the theater in tears.

3. **mortify:** (adj.) dead to the world; deadened; destroyed.
   Example: Driving a stake through the heart of the vampire *mortified* it.

4. **gentry:** (n.) rank according to birth; nobility, nobles.
   Example: When the British monarchs attend the races at Ascot, they're often surrounded by the *gentry*.

5. **distempered:** (adj.) disordered; deranged; disturbed.
   Example: The sudden killing spree seemed to be the work of a *distempered* mind.

6. **upbraid:** (v.) to bring forward as grounds or basis for censure.
   Example: Vowing not to allow re-election, the angry voters *upbraided* the political candidate for not taking a definite stand on specific issues.

7. **skirr:** (v.) to fly, whir, scour.
   Example: The small child *skirred* the house looking for the Christmas presents that his parents had hidden.

8. **raze:** (v.) to obliterate; destroy completely.
   Example: The construction of the new dormitory *razed* seven historic homes that once stood on the block.

9. **pristine:** (adj.) having original purity; uncontaminated.
   Example: With lots of care and hard work, the man was able to restore the old table to *pristine* condition.

scene v

10. **treatise:** (n.) tale; talk.
    Example: When camping as children, my father and uncles enjoyed *treatises* about local ghosts.

Prereading Activity
for
Macbeth
Plot Summaries
Act V

Directions: To help you better understand and follow *Macbeth,* read the summary of a specific scene before you begin to read it. If you get lost during the scene, you can refer to the summary.

Act V, scene i

In Macbeth's castle at Dunsinane, the gentlewoman and the Scottish Doctor discuss what they have seen for the previous two nights as Lady Macbeth has sleepwalked. Lady Macbeth has taken out paper, written a letter, sealed it, and then returned to bed. The doctor asks if Lady Macbeth has said anything. The gentlewoman is reluctant to report what she's heard, for she has no other witness to substantiate it.

A sleepwalking Lady Macbeth enters, carrying a candle. In her sleep she seems to be washing her hands, something that the gentlewoman says is her usual behavior. As Lady Macbeth speaks, the doctor writes down what he hears.

In her dreams, Lady Macbeth reviews what she and Macbeth have done. She tries to wash the spots of blood from her hands. She rebukes Macbeth for his cowardice about killing Duncan. Then she recalls the murder of Lady Macduff (wife of Thane of Fife). She returns to the blood on her hands that will not come out.

The doctor concludes that Lady Macbeth's heart is heavy with guilt and that he cannot help her.

When Lady Macbeth speaks again, she tells her husband to wash his hands and get ready for bed; Banquo's dead and can't harm him; there's a knocking at the gate; what's done is done.

The doctor concludes that Lady Macbeth will confess in her sleep the unnatural acts that she committed while awake. The doctor tells the gentlewoman to look after Lady Macbeth and to remove her from anything that annoys her. Although the doctor has witnessed Lady Macbeth's sleepwalking, he fears saying anything.

Act V, scene ii

In the country near Dunsinane, Menteith, Caithness, Angus, and Lennox have come with their armies. They plan to meet with the English forces led by Malcolm, his uncle Siward, and Macduff near Birnam Wood. Donalbain is not with his brother.

They know that Macbeth has fortified the castle at Dunsinane and many rumor that he is mad or at least in a fury because his reign of terror can no longer control the country. Macbeth now commands through fear rather than through inspiring loyalty. Knowing that the cause is just, they march to Birnam Wood.

Act V, scene iii

Inside the castle at Dunsinane, Macbeth feels invincible and wants no more reports. He won't be afraid until Birnam Wood moves on Dunsinane. He scoffs at Malcolm who's a boy born of a woman, and the English forces.

A frightened servant enters and tells Macbeth that the English forces number 10,000.

Macbeth realizes that he may well be defeated. He calls Seton, who confirms the report. Macbeth vows to fight till the end. He calls for his armor, and then asks the doctor about Lady Macbeth. The doctor tells Macbeth that she is not sick of body but of mind, and that only she can cure that.

Macbeth reminds even the doctor that they have nothing to fear until the woods march on the castle.

Act V, scene iv

The Scottish armies meet the English forces headed by Malcolm, Macduff, Siward, and young Siward. To disguise the size of the army until they are close enough to attack, Malcolm orders all the soldiers to carry tree branches from Birnam Wood, thus fulfilling the prophecy of the witches' third apparition.

Act V, scene v

Within the castle, Macbeth awaits a siege. A woman cries offstage and Seton goes to investigate. He returns with the news that Lady Macbeth is dead. Macbeth realizes the mortality of existence and the monotony of life. A dumbfounded messenger comes in and tells Macbeth that he saw Birnam Wood marching towards the castle. The news angers Macbeth but also moves him to action.

Act V, scene vi

Outside the castle, the armies discard their branches. Malcolm maps out the plan of attack: first Siward and his son, then Macduff, and finally Malcolm's forces.

Act V, scene vii

Inside the castle, Macbeth's forces are losing and the odds so overwhelm him that he feels like a bear tied to a stake. Young Siward enters, and Macbeth kills him. With his victory, Macbeth feels that the prophecy of the second apparition has come true: Young Siward, a man born of woman, could not harm him. Macbeth then leaves.

Macduff enters ready to avenge the murder of his family. He's followed by Malcolm and Siward.

Act V, scene viii

Macduff encounters Macbeth. They fight. Believing he's protected by the prophecy that no man born of woman can harm him, he scoffs at Macduff's efforts. Then Macduff informs Macbeth that he was not born in the normal fashion, but delivered by Caesarean section. Macbeth realizes that his life is not charmed, but he vows to fight valiantly.

Act V, scene ix

After the battle, Malcolm is victorious. Ross informs the assembled generals that young Siward has died as a valiant soldier. Macduff enters, carrying Macbeth's head. Malcolm rewards the Scottish nobles with new titles as Earls. He also tells the audience that Lady Macbeth committed suicide. Now that the rightful monarchy is restored, Malcolm plans to recall all whom Macbeth exiled, and restore order and peace to Scotland.

Class Period:

CHARACTER ASSIGNMENTS FOR ORAL READING GROUPS
Macbeth

Session 7: Act V, scenes i, ii, iii, iv

Characters	*Group 1*	*Group 2*	*Group 3*	*Group 4*
Doctor, Lennox, Siward	___	___	___	___
Gentlewoman	___	___	___	___
Lady Macbeth	___	___	___	___
Menteith, Macduff	___	___	___	___
Angus, Soldiers	___	___	___	___
Caithness, Servant	___	___	___	___
Macbeth	___	___	___	___
Seton, Malcolm	___	___	___	___

Class Period:

CHARACTER ASSIGNMENTS FOR ORAL READING GROUPS
Macbeth

Session 8: Act V, scenes v, vi, vii, viii, ix

Characters	*Group 1*	*Group 2*	*Group 3*	*Group 4*
Malcolm	___	___	___	___
Siward	___	___	___	___
Macduff	___	___	___	___
Macbeth	___	___	___	___
Young Siward	___	___	___	___
Ross	___	___	___	___
Seton	___	___	___	___
Messenger	___	___	___	___

180

NAME:_____   DATE:_____

During-reading Activity
for
Macbeth
Character Diary 7
Act V, scenes i, ii, iii, iv

Directions: Use the space below to record your character's reactions to the events in the first four scenes in Act V of *Macbeth*. Remember to include a summary of events, explain how your character learned of them, and give your character's reactions to them. Because this act has nine scenes, you may want to record your character's entries as you read each scene. If you need additional room, use the back of this sheet.

The Personal Diary of

_____
(character's name)

A few months after Act IV

_____
_____
_____
_____
_____
_____
_____
_____
_____
_____
_____
_____
_____
_____
_____
_____

During-reading Activity
for
Macbeth
Character Diary 8
Act V, scenes v, vi, vii, viii, ix

Directions: Use the space below to record your character's reactions to the events of the last five scenes in Act V of *Macbeth*. Remember to include a summary of events, explain how your character learned of them, and give your character's reactions to them. Because this act has nine scenes, you may want to record your character's entries as you read each scene. If you need additional room, use the back of this sheet.

The Personal Diary of

_____
(character's name)

Later that day

_____
_____
_____
_____
_____
_____
_____
_____
_____
_____
_____
_____
_____
_____

NAME:_____   DATE:_____

During-reading Activity
for
Macbeth
Viewing Act V, scene i
Lady Macbeth Sleepwalks

Directions: After you've read this scene, viewing a film or video version may help you better understand how the text translates into the characters' actions. Although you may want to keep your copy of the play handy, don't be surprised if the actors' script varies from yours. Film scripts often delete or reorder the lines in the play. You many want to note questions you need to ask your teacher afterwards. After viewing the scene, take a few minutes to respond to the questions below.

1. Besides speaking the lines, what does Lady Macbeth do that reveals her guilt to the doctor and gentlewoman?

2. How do the gentlewoman and the doctor react to Lady Macbeth's behavior?

3. How do the lighting and sound effects enhance the mood of this scene?

During-reading Activity
for
Macbeth
Guide to Character Development: Macbeth
Act V

Shakespeare reveals his characters in four ways:

ૐ through what the characters say to other characters in dialogue;

ૐ through what the characters reveal about their thoughts through long speeches to the audience called *soliloquies;*

ૐ through what other characters say about them;

ૐ through what they do, their actions.

As you read the play, examine the following scenes for what they reveal about Macbeth's character and fill in the chart briefly using your own words. If you need more room, use the back of the page.

Scene	*What Macbeth says, does, or what others say about him*	*What this reveals about Macbeth's character*
Act V, scene iii Macbeth learns that the English forces number 10,000		
Act V, scene iii Doctor informs Macbeth that Lady Macbeth's illness is in her mind		
Act V, scene v Lady Macbeth dies		

© 1994 by The Center for Applied Research in Education

Act V, scene v Messenger reports that Birnam Wood is marching on the castle		
Act V, scene vii Macbeth kills young Siward		
Act V, scene viii Macbeth learns that Macduff is not "a man of woman born"		

NAME:_____   DATE:_____

During-reading Activity
for
Macbeth
Guide to Character Development: Lady Macbeth
Act V

Shakespeare reveals his characters in four ways:

- ❧ through what the characters say to other characters in dialogue;
- ❧ through what the characters reveal about their thoughts through long speeches to the audience called *soliloquies;*
- ❧ through what other characters say about them;
- ❧ through what they do, their actions.

As you read the play, examine the following scenes for what they reveal about Lady Macbeth's character and fill in the chart briefly using your own words. If you need more room, use the back of the page.

Scene	What Lady Macbeth says, does, or what others say about her	What this reveals about Lady Macbeth's character
Act V, scene i The Scottish doctor and the gentlewoman observe Lady Macbeth's sleepwalking		
Act V, scene v Lady Macbeth dies		

© 1994 by The Center for Applied Research in Education

NAME:_____   DATE:_____

During-reading Activity
for
Macbeth
Guide to Character Development: Macduff
Act V

Shakespeare reveals his characters in four ways:

- ❧ through what the characters say to other characters in dialogue;
- ❧ through what the characters reveal about their thoughts through long speeches to the audience called *soliloquies;*
- ❧ through what other characters say about them;
- ❧ through what they do, their actions.

As you read the play, examine the following scenes for what they reveal about Macduff's character and fill in the chart briefly using your own words. If you need more room, use the back of the page.

Scene	*What Macduff says, does, or what others say about him*	*What this reveals about Macduff's character*
Act V, scene iv The Scottish and English armies join forces near Birnam Wood		
Act V, scene vi Macduff sounds the attack against Macbeth		
Act V, scene viii Macbeth learns that Macduff is not "a man of woman born"		

During-reading Activity
for
Macbeth
Guide to Character Development: Ross
Act V

Shakespeare reveals his characters in four ways:

❧ through what the characters say to other characters in dialogue;
❧ through what the characters reveal about their thoughts through long speeches to the audience called *soliloquies;*
❧ through what other characters say about them;
❧ through what they do, their actions.

As you read the play, examine the following scene for what it reveals about Ross's character and fill in the chart briefly using your own words. If you need more room, use the back of the page.

Scene	What Ross says, does, or what others say about him	What this reveals about Ross's character
Act V, scene ix Ross reveals that Macbeth killed young Siward		

© 1994 by The Center for Applied Research in Education

NAME:_____   DATE:_____

During-reading Activity
for
Macbeth
Guide to Character Development: Malcolm
Act V

Shakespeare reveals his characters in four ways:

- through what the characters say to other characters in dialogue;
- through what the characters reveal about their thoughts through long speeches to the audience called *soliloquies;*
- through what other characters say about them;
- through what they do, their actions.

As you read the play, examine the following scenes for what they reveal about Malcolm's character and fill in the chart briefly using your own words. If you need more room, use the back of the page.

Scene	What Malcolm does, says, or what others say about him	What this reveals about Malcolm's character
Act V, scene iv The Scottish and English armies join forces near Birnam Wood		
Act V, scene vi Malcolm plans the attack		
Act V, scene ix Malcolm thanks his nobles		

Postreading Activity
for
Macbeth
Comprehension Check
Act V

Directions: After you've read all of Act V, use the following questions to check how well you've understood what you've read. For each question, select the most appropriate answer from the choices listed below it. Place the letter corresponding to your answer in the space to the left of the item number.

____1. Why won't the gentlewoman report what Lady Macbeth says while sleepwalking?

    A. Because she can't hear what Lady Macbeth says.
    B. Because she doesn't have a witness to verify her testimony.
    C. Because she is afraid Lady Macbeth will kill her.
    D. Because she is afraid Macbeth will kill her.
    E. Because she is sworn to secrecy.

____2. How does Birnam Wood march to Dunsinane?

    A. The witches make the trees move.
    B. Malcolm's armies cut down the trees.
    C. Malcolm's army uses branches to camouflage their numbers.
    D. Macbeth's army cuts down the trees.
    E. An earthquake uproots the trees.

____3. What does the audience learn from Lady Macbeth's sleepwalking scene?

    A. That she is insane.
    B. That she killed Duncan.
    C. That she shares the guilt for all that Macbeth has done.
    D. That she blames Macbeth for her problems.
    E. That she is the evil force behind Macbeth and must bear all the blame alone.

_____4. What does Macduff mean when he tells Macbeth,

&

Despair thy charm,
And let the angel whom thou still hast served
Tell thee, Macduff was from his mother's womb
Untimely ripped.

&

A. That Macduff also has a charmed life because he's also seen the witches.
B. That Macbeth is about to die.
C. That Macduff will kill Macbeth.
D. That Macduff was not born in the usual manner.
E. That Macduff will surrender.

_____5. What weakness in Macbeth's character makes it possible for the prophecies to come true and defeat him?

A. Macbeth interprets the prophecies too literally.
B. Macbeth doesn't believe in witchcraft.
C. Macbeth is insane.
D. Macbeth underestimates Macduff's skill as a soldier.
E. Macbeth is consumed with his own guilt.

Postreading Activity
for
Macbeth
Small Group Discussion to Check Comprehension
Act V

Directions: After you've read all of Act V, discuss each of the following questions in small groups briefly. Use the space below each question to note points you may want to share later. If you need more room, use the back of the page.

1.   What scenes or events does Lady Macbeth refer to during her sleep-walking?

2.   How does Malcolm make the prophecy about Birnam Wood marching on Dunsinane come true?

3.   What seems to be the reason for Lady Macbeth's sleepwalking?

4.   What doesn't Macbeth know about Macduff that should make Macbeth fear him?

5.   What weaknesses in Macbeth's character help the prophecies come true?

Postreading Activity
for
Macbeth
Critical Thinking Questions
Act V

Directions: To help you develop your understanding of Act V, as your teacher directs you, take time to think about and discuss the following questions. The first question is the focus question and is the point of the discussion. Don't be concerned that you may not be able to answer this question at first. Proceed to the exploration questions and then return to the focus question.

Focus Question. Why do you think that Macbeth insists on fighting Macduff to the bitter end when he already acknowledges that much of what he's done is evil?

Exploration Questions.

1. Although Macbeth knows he has no heir, what leads Macbeth to believe that he's still invincible?

2. What other characters in literature have believed they were invincible but have been defeated ultimately?

3. Why do you believe that the play does (or does not) reach a just ending?

4. What makes one person's death a tragedy while another person's death may be considered unfortunate?

5. What evidence within the play suggests that Macbeth will be defeated ultimately?

6. Why would contemporary society feel that Macbeth's defeat and death is just?

Postreading Activity
for
Macbeth
Language Exploration
Irony
Act V

Imagine that while you're in the school cafeteria, someone drops his tray. One of your friends begins applauding and yells out "Way to go, Grace!" More than likely, you'll probably begin to laugh because there's a discrepancy between what your friend said and what she meant. Dropping the tray is not a sign of graceful coordination. When we say one thing and mean another, it is an example of *verbal irony*. Verbal irony is often used in literature. Either the author or a character may say one thing and mean another. This is often the case in Shakespeare's plays.

For example, in *Macbeth,* Act I, scene iii, Banquo cautions Macbeth about the witches' prophecies:

ɚ

But 'tis strange:
And oftentimes, to win us to our harm,
The instruments of darkness tell us truths,

ɚ

In these lines, Banquo warns Macbeth about how truth can bring harm. It is true that Macbeth becomes King, but he must murder the rightful king to achieve the position.

Shakespeare also uses *situational irony*. Situational irony occurs when a discrepancy exists between what a character says and what a character does, or a discrepancy between what a character expects to happen and what does happen. For example, in Act I, scene iii, Macbeth learns that he is now Thane of Cawdor and wonders about the prophecy of his becoming king:

ɚ

If good, why do I yield to that suggestion,
Whose horrid image doth unfix my hair,
And make my seated heart knock at my ribs
Against the use of nature.

ɚ

The irony here is that while Macbeth is pleased with his good fortune to become Thane of Cawdor, he is uneasy about his possibly becoming king.

© 1994 by The Center for Applied Research in Education

Directions: The following passages contain examples of verbal and situational irony. Working in pairs, small groups, or as your teacher directs, review each passage in the context of the play and determine the difference between what is said or done and what is expected.

1. Duncan describing Inverness when he arrives (Act I, scene vi):

    ❧

    This castle hath a pleasant seat; the air
    Nimbly and sweetly recommends itself
    Unto our gentle senses.

    ❧

2. Lady Macbeth welcoming Duncan (Act I, scene vi):

    ❧

              All our service
    In every point twice done, and then done double,
    Were poor and single business, to contend
    Against those honors deep and broad wherewith
    Your majesty loads our house.

    ❧

3. Lady Macbeth commenting upon her drugging of the King's guards (Act II, scene ii):

    ❧

    That which hath made them drunk has made me bold.
    What hath quenched them hath given me fire.

    ❧

© 1994 by The Center for Applied Research in Education

4. Lady Macbeth fearing that Macbeth might fail (Act II, scene ii):

Alack, I am afraid they have awaked,
And 'tis not done. Th' attempt, and not the deed,
Confounds us. Hark! I laid their daggers ready,
He could not miss 'em—Had he not resembled
My father as he slept, I had done't.

5. Macbeth commenting on meeting the guards after he killed Duncan (Act II, scene ii):

One cried, God bless us, and, Amen the other,
As they had seen me with these hangman's hands.
Listening their fear, I could not say, Amen,
When they did say, God bless us!

6. Banquo to his son (Act III, scene iii):

O treachery! Fly good Fleance, fly, fly, fly!
Thou mayst revenge. O slave!

7. Second Witch (Act IV, scene i):

    By the pricking of my thumbs,
    Something wicked this way comes.

8. Second Apparition (Act IV, scene i):

    Be bloody, bold, and resolute; laugh to scan
    The power of man. For none of women born
    Shall harm Macbeth.

9. Third Apparition (Act IV, scene i):

    Macbeth shall never vanquished be until
    Great Birnam wood to high Dunsinane Hill
    Shall come against him.

10. Macduff to Macbeth (Act V, scene vii):

    Despair thy charm,
    And let the angel whom thou still hast served
    Tell thee, Macduff was from his mother's womb
    Untimely ripped.

Language Exploration Review
Macbeth

Directions: Now that you've discussed all the Language Exploration Activities, use the following questions to check how well you can apply what you've learned to new selections. For each question, select the most appropriate answer from the choices listed below it. Place the letter corresponding to your answer in the space to the left of the item number.

Questions 1 and 2 refer to the following passage:

❧

> . . . .*O nation miserable,*
> *With an untitled tyrant bloody-sceptered,*
> *When shalt thou see thy wholesome days again,*
> *Since that the truest issue of thy throne*
> *By his own interdiction stands accursed,*
> *And does blaspheme his breed?*

❧

_____1.   Which of the following literary devices is Macduff using?

A. metaphor   B. personification   C. alliteration   D. simile   E. irony

_____2.   In the passage, Macduff questions

A. Whether Macbeth's tyranny is worse than Duncan's.
B. Whether Malcolm is the rightful king.
C. Whether the people of Scotland can ever be happy without the rightful king ruling.
D. Whether the people will ever be free of Macbeth's tyranny.
E. How miserable the country is.

Questions 3 and 4 refer to the following passage from Act V, scene vii:

❧

> *They have tied me to a stake; I cannot fly,*
> *But bear-like I must fight the course.*

❧

_____3.   Which of the following literary devices is Macbeth using in the first line?

A. simile   B. personification   C. apostrophe   D. metaphor   E. irony

198

© 1994 by The Center for Applied Research in Education

_____4. Which does Macbeth imply about the effect of the attack upon him?

A. He's stubborn.
B. He's ignorant.
C. He's innocent.
D. He's trapped.
E. He's angry.

Questions 5 and 6 refer to the following passage:

&

We have scotched the snake, not killed it.
She'll close, and be herself, whilst our poor malice
Remains in danger of her former tooth.

&

_____5. Which of the following literary devices is Macbeth using?

A. metaphor   B. alliteration   C. apostrophe   D. simile   E. symbol

_____6. In this passage, Macbeth suggests

A. That his position is only secure temporarily.
B. That he is a snake.
C. That he is in complete control.
D. That he is resourceful.
E. That he is free.

Questions 7 and 8 refer to the following passage where Banquo reflects upon the truth of the witches' prophecies (Act III, scene i):

&

. . . .If there come truth from them,
As upon thee Macbeth, their speeches shine,
Why by the verities on thee made good
May they not be my oracles as well,
And set me up in hope?

&

_____7. Which sense does the passage appeal to?

A. touch   B. smell   C. taste   D. sight   E. hearing

____8.   In the passage, what does Banquo suggest?

A. That Macbeth is a fraud.
B. That the witches' prophecy about Banquo will come true, too.
C. That Macbeth is evil.
D. That Banquo will become king.
E. That Banquo should murder Macbeth.

Questions 9 and 10 refer to the following passage:

‿

Macbeth shall never vanquished be until
Great Birnam wood to high Dunsinane Hill
Shall come against him.

‿

____9.   Which of the following literary devices does Shakespeare use **here**?
A. irony   B. alliteration   C. apostrophe   D. simile   E. symbol

____10. Why isn't Macbeth concerned about this vision?

A. He has a charmed life.
B. He has Macduff as a friend.
C. The vision involves witchcraft.
D. The vision foretells his own death.
E. The vision seems impossible.

Postreading Activity
for
Macbeth
Vocabulary in Context
Act V

Directions: In each of the passages below you will find one of the words from the prereading vocabulary list for Act V. Review the definitions given in the prereading vocabulary. Working individually, in pairs, or in small groups as your teacher directs, examine each of the underlined words in the following passages from Act V. For each word, use the appropriate meaning and develop a brief interpretation of the passage within the context of the play.

1. Doctor commenting upon Lady Macbeth's sleepwalking (scene i):

    ❧

    A great perturbation in nature, to receive at once the benefit of sleep, and do the effects of watching.

    ❧

2. Doctor commenting on why Lady Macbeth sleepwalks (scene i):

    ❧

    What a sigh is here! The heart is sorely charged.

    ❧

3. Menteith commenting upon Macduff and Malcolm's reasons for revenge (scene ii):

&

Revenges burn in them; for their dear causes
Would to the bleeding and the grim alarm
Excite the <u>mortified</u> man.

&

4. Lennox acknowledging the nobles who have joined with Malcolm and Macduff (scene ii):

&

. . . .I have a file
Of all the <u>gentry</u>; there is Siward's son,
And many unrough youths, that even now
Protest their first of manhood.

&

5. Caithness reporting on Macbeth's state of mind (scene ii):

&

Some say he is mad; others, that lesser hate him,
Do call it valiant fury, but for certain
He cannot buckle his <u>distempered</u> cause
Within his belt of rule.

&

6.   Angus reporting Macbeth's inability to lead (scene ii):

ﶞ

Now minutely revolts <u>upbraid</u> his faith-breach;
Those he commands move only in command,
Nothing in love.

ﶞ

7.   Macbeth ordering Seton (scene iii):

ﶞ

Send out moe horses, <u>skirr</u> the country round,
Hang those that talk of fear.

ﶞ

8.   Macbeth questioning the doctor's ability to cure Lady **Macbeth** (scene iii):

ﶞ

Cure her of that.
Canst thou not minister to a mind diseased,
Pluck from the memory a rooted sorrow,
<u>Raze</u> out the written troubles of the brain,

ﶞ

9.   Macbeth urging the doctor for a cure of his wife (scene iii):

                               ઢ

> . . . .*If thou couldst, doctor, cast*
> *The water of my land, find her disease,*
> *And purge it to a sound and <u>pristine</u> health*

                               ઢ

10.   Macbeth reacting to the cries of women offstage (scene v):

                               ઢ

> *The time has been, my senses would have cooled*
> *To hear a night-shriek, and fell of hair*
> *Would at a dismal <u>treatise</u> rouse and stir*
> *As life were in't.*

                               ઢ

NAME:_____   DATE:_____

Vocabulary Review Quiz
for
Macbeth
Act V

Directions: For each of the italicized words in the sentences below, determine which letter best reflects the use of the word in its context. Place the letter corresponding to your answer in the space to the left of the item number.

_____1. When the doctor says that Lady Macbeth's sleepwalking is due to a *perturbation,* he means

A. emotional upset   B. character defect   C. mental agitation
D. little annoyance   E. temporary insanity

_____2. To say that Lady Macbeth's heart is "sorely *charged*" means

A. overwrought   B. full of compassion   C. full of anger
D. suffused with emotion   E. concerned for her husband's welfare

_____3. As Menteith uses the term, a *mortified* man would be one

A. who's embarrassed   B. who's uncaring   C. who's dead
D. who's understanding   E. who's deaf

_____4. The *gentry* are

A. the rebels   B. the royal household   C. the middle class
D. the peasants   E. the nobility

_____5. When Caithness refers to Macbeth's *distempered* cause, he means it is

A. greedy   B. insane   C. inconsistent   D. overwhelming   E. disturbed

_____6. When Angus reports that small revolts *upbraid* Macbeth, he means they

A. censure Macbeth   B. bring forth grounds for censure of Macbeth
C. point out all his evil doings   D. create more problems for Macbeth
E. will dethrone Macbeth

_____7. When Macbeth orders the country to be *skirred,* he means
A. scrubbed   B. edged   C. scoured   D. destroyed   E. overthrown

_____8. When Macbeth asks the doctor to *raze* Lady Macbeth's madness, he means

A. obliterate   B. build   C. cease   D. cure   E. find the cause

_____9. *Pristine* means

A. restored   B. pure   C. snobbish   D. straightforward   E. unwilling

_____10. When Macbeth refers to a dismal *treatise,* he means

A. a tale or story   B. an essay   C. a long argument   D. a brief chat
E. an elaborately constructed epic

EXTENDING ACTIVITIES

Overview of
Extending Activities
for
Macbeth

Directions: Now that you've completed your formal study of *Macbeth*, the extending activities listed below will provide you with opportunities to extend your understanding of the play. Remember that these are suggestions of things you might do. Perhaps you will think of others or your teacher may have additional suggestions. Your teacher can provide you with specific sets of directions for *acting out, oral interpretation, puppet theater, masks, writing assignments,* and *visual displays.*

Acting Out:

   1.   Dramatize a missing scene related to the characters and situations in the play. For example, after Macbeth's second visit to the witches, how does he explain the apparitions to Lady Macbeth?

   2.   Present a scene from the play in a modern context. Use contemporary settings, words, and ideas. For example, what might Macbeth's "Is this a dagger" soliloquy sound like as a rap lyric?

Oral Interpretation   Present a prepared reading of the speech of a single character, between two characters, or of an entire scene. Keep in mind that oral interpretation involves communicating the words effectively *without* actually memorizing a script and acting out a scene with full costumes and props.

Puppet Theater   Make paper bag puppets and use them to present a scene from the play.

Masks   Create paper plate masks for specific characters and present a scene from the play using them.

Writing Assignments

   1.   Write an alternative ending to the play.

   2.   Research some element of Scottish life in the time of Macbeth (1200 A.D.) or the time of Shakespeare (approximately 1600 A.D.)

   3.   Using the character diary you kept while reading the play, write a letter or note from your character to another character in the play or to a relative from a neighboring country.

Visual
Displays

1. Create a graffiti wall for Inverness, Fife, or Dunsinane castles that reflects a specific time during the play.

2. Create a time line for the play where you list the significant events in order.

3. Draw a comic strip or drawing of a scene from the play.

4. Create a filmstrip or video related to the play.

5. Construct a mobile using double-sided objects/characters from the play with a 3 x 5 card containing a description beneath each object.

6. Create a music video combining still pictures with music and words.

7. Select and depict 12 to 16 scenes from the play for a multiple-panel quilt. Make each panel out of paper. For each panel of your quilt, create an illustration and write a caption that explains it. Create a border for each panel and tie or string them together using clothesline or heavy string to form a large wall hanging.

8. Research and build a Globe Theater model.

9. Research and present samples of Scottish cooking.

10. Research and present how Elizabethan actors may have interpreted Scottish costumes.

11. Create a slide sound presentation on some aspect of the play.

Extending Activities
for
Macbeth
Acting Out

Directions: From time to time during your study of *Macbeth,* you may have participated in an improvised scene from the play either before or after you read particular scenes. Now that you've read the entire play, here are some additional opportunities for you to act out and demonstrate your fuller understanding of the play and its characters. You may want to improvise these scenes or to fully script and rehearse them.

1. Suppose you were the two guards outside Duncan's chamber. While Macbeth is murdering Duncan, what do you hear that causes you to say a prayer?

2. Suppose you were the two guards outside Duncan's chamber. How do you try to defend yourselves when Macbeth accuses you of murdering the king?

3. Ross and Lennox discuss King Macbeth's strange behavior after the banquet (Act III, scene iv).

4. As the three witches just prior to Hecate's appearance (Act III, scene v), you begin to brag to your fellow witches about how you've meddled in Macbeth's life and condemned his soul. You may want to end with a modern paraphrased version of Hecate's speech.

5. After the end of the play, Malcolm appears before the people to let them know that he is King of Scotland. What does he say?

6. Create a scene in Heaven or Hell where specific characters defend their lives or tell others what has happened in their lives. You may want to include Macbeth along with the other characters in the play.

'7. As Banquo's heir, Fleance will become king after Malcolm. Create the scene similar to the end of Act I, scene iv, where an older Malcolm names Fleance his heir and explains why.

8. Lady Macbeth's mother comes for the coronation of King Macbeth. In private, what does she say to her daughter about the events that have led up to Macbeth's becoming king?

9. Develop a segment for "60 Minutes," CBS NBC, or ABC Evening News, "Entertainment Tonight," "Phil Donahue," "Oprah," "Geraldo," "Now It Can Be Told," or "A Current Affair" based upon *Macbeth.*

10. The porter who opens the gate for Macduff and Lennox tells his wife about the events surrounding Duncan's murder.

NAME:_____   DATE:_____

Extending Activity
for
Macbeth
Oral Interpretation

Directions: Present a prepared reading of a speech or scene from *Macbeth*. Listed below are suggestions of scenes for one, two, three, or four actors to choose from. You may want to check with your teacher to present other scenes as well. To help you prepare for your scene, work through all the steps.

*Scenes for
Solo Actors:*

Lady Macbeth, Act I, scene v—She reads Macbeth's letter and contemplates its meaning

Macbeth, Act I, scene vii—Macbeth's soliloquy, "If it were done. . ."

Macbeth, Act II, scene ii—Macbeth's soliloquy, "Is this a dagger. . ."

Hecate, Act III, scene v—"Have I not reason. . ."

*Scenes for
Two Actors:*

Macbeth, Lady Macbeth, Act I, scene v—Macbeth and Lady Macbeth consider murdering Duncan

Macbeth, Lady Macbeth, Act I, scene vii—Lady Macbeth convinces Macbeth to kill Duncan

Macbeth, Lady Macbeth, Act II, scene ii— Macbeth and Lady Macbeth react to murdering Duncan

Ross and Old Man, Act II, scene iv—Discussion of Duncan's murder

Macbeth and Lady Macbeth, Act III, scene ii—Macbeth doesn't tell Lady Macbeth about plot to murder Banquo and Fleance

Lennox and Lord, Act III, scene vi—Discussion of Macbeth's tyranny

Macbeth and Macduff, Act V, scene ix—Final confrontation

*Scenes for Three
or More Actors:*

Malcolm, Captain, Duncan, Act I, scene ii—Wounded captain's description of the battle

Malcolm, Ross, Angus, Lennox, Duncan, Act I, scene ii—Ross's description of the battle at Fife

Macbeth, Banquo, the witches, Act I, scene iii—Macbeth's first encounter with the witches

Macbeth, Banquo, Ross, and Angus, Act I, scene iii—Angus and Ross bring Macbeth word of his new title

Duncan, Malcolm, Macbeth, Banquo, Act I, scene iv—Duncan thanks Macbeth formally

Macbeth, Lady Macbeth, Banquo, Act III, scene i—Macbeth invites Banquo to banquet

Macbeth, First Murderer, Second Murderer, Act III, scene i—Macbeth orders Banquo and Fleance's murder

Macbeth, Lady Macbeth, Murderer, Lennox, Ross, Act III, scene iv—Macbeth confronts Banquo's ghost

Macbeth, three Witches, Lennox, Act IV, scene i—Macbeth returns to witches

Malcolm, Macduff, Ross, English Doctor, Act IV, scene iii—Macduff urges Malcolm to oppose Macbeth

Doctor, Gentlewoman, Lady Macbeth, Act V, scene i—Lady Macbeth sleepwalks

Macbeth, Seton, Messenger, Act V, scene v—Birnam Wood marches on Dunsinane

Steps for Preparing an Oral Interpretation:

1. Select a scene or passage that you really like. The passage should have a definite beginning, high point, and an end. Remember that you will be doing a prepared reading and not memorizing a script. Most often oral interpreters either stand before their audience or sit on a stool.

2. Prepare a script to work from. You may want to type out the selection or Xerox it from a book. You'll need a copy that you can make notes on. Mount your script on black construction paper, so you can read from it easily without having to hold it with both hands. Keep the pages of your manuscript loose, so you can either slide them out of the way or shift them under each other as you finish reading them.

3. Analyze the script. As you work through the analysis, make notes to yourself in pencil on your script.

   a. Read the whole passage and decide what it's about. Because you've already read the whole play, you know where your selection fits into the development of the characters.

213

© 1994 by The Center for Applied Research in Education

    b.   Read the whole piece several times and decide what the overall effect of the piece is.

    c.   Make notes of things you don't understand—allusions, words, and so forth. Check the footnotes in your text or look up unfamiliar words in the dictionary. Remember that the meaning of particular words may have changed since Shakespeare's time. If you have a problem understanding a particular word, check glossary of terms found in most *Complete Works of Shakespeare* plays in your library.

    d.   As you look at individual words, you should know how to pronounce all of them as well as know both their *denotative* meaning (the dictionary meaning) and their *connotative* meaning (the emotional subtleties that come from using the word in a particular context).

    e.   Where does the scene take place? Is it a public place, like the great hall of the castle, or a private one like Lady Macbeth's chamber? Who speaks here and what is the speaker's emotional state at the time? What has happened before this scene?

    f.   Examine the overall organization of the scene. What emotions do the characters reveal? What changes in character, motivation, or emotions occur during the scene? In Act I, scene iv, Duncan shifts from thanking Macbeth and Banquo to naming Malcolm his heir. Decide how you can convey these changes with your voice.

4.   Begin practicing aloud. Read the passage out loud, working either with a partner or with a tape recorder. Listen to yourself. Experiment with different readings. Underline words you want to emphasize. Make marginal notes about the emotions you would like to portray in different parts.

5.   Write a brief introduction to your scene, setting it up for your listeners. The following example could be used to introduce Act I, scene v:

Although Macbeth had previously agreed to his wife's plan to murder the king, while at the banquet for Duncan, Macbeth has second thoughts and leaves the Great Hall, followed closely by his wife.

6.   Once you've decided on how you would like to read your selection, practice, practice, practice! Your goal in these sessions is not to memorize the words but to learn the interpretation, so that when you present it, you can concentrate on a smooth performance.

7.   Perform the piece. Some interpreters prefer to stand while others prefer to sit upon stools. You may hold the script in your hands or use a music stand or lectern.

NAME:_____   DATE:_____

Extending Activity
for
Macbeth
Puppet Theater

One way to present scenes from *Macbeth* without having to worry about elaborate sets or costumes is to use puppets made from brown paper bags. You can make your own puppets using construction paper, scissors, rubber cement, crayons, and felt-tip markers. You can use a table turned sideways as a stage for the puppeteers to hide behind. If you feel that you need scenery, make a mural and use masking tape to secure it to the wall behind you.

*Steps to Making
and Performing Scene
with Puppets:*

1. Select a scene that you want to perform. Listed below are scenes for two, three, or more actors.

*Scenes for
Two Actors:*

Macbeth, Lady Macbeth, Act I, scene v—Macbeth and Lady Macbeth consider murdering Duncan

Macbeth, Lady Macbeth, Act I, scene vii—Lady Macbeth convinces Macbeth to kill Duncan

Macbeth, Lady Macbeth, Act II, scene ii— Macbeth and Lady Macbeth react to murdering Duncan

Ross and Old Man, Act II, scene iv—Discussion of Duncan's murder

Macbeth and Lady Macbeth, Act III, scene ii—Macbeth doesn't tell Lady Macbeth about plot to murder Banquo and Fleance

Lennox and Lord, Act III, scene vi—Discussion of Macbeth's tyranny

Macbeth and Macduff, Act V, scene ix—Final confrontation

*Scenes for
Three or
More Actors:*

Malcolm, Captain, Duncan, Act I, scene ii—Wounded captain's description of the battle

Malcolm, Ross, Angus, Lennox, Duncan, Act I, scene ii—Ross's description of the battle at Fife

Macbeth, Banquo, the witches, Act I, scene iii—Macbeth's first encounter with the witches

Macbeth, Banquo, Ross, and Angus, Act I, scene iii—Angus and Ross bring Macbeth word of his new title

Duncan, Malcolm, Macbeth, Banquo, Act I, scene iv—Duncan thanks Macbeth formally

Macbeth, Lady Macbeth, Banquo, Act III, scene i—Macbeth invites Banquo to banquet

Macbeth, First Murderer, Second Murderer, Act III, scene i—Macbeth orders Banquo and Fleance's murder

Macbeth, Lady Macbeth, Murderer, Lennox, Ross, Act III, scene iv—Macbeth confronts Banquo's ghost

Macbeth, three Witches, Lennox, Act IV, scene i—Macbeth returns to witches

Malcolm, Macduff, Ross, English Doctor, Act IV, scene iii—Macduff urges Malcolm to oppose Macbeth

Doctor, Gentlewoman, Lady Macbeth, Act V, scene i—Lady Macbeth sleepwalks

Macbeth, Seton, Messenger, Act V, scene v—Birnam Wood marches on Dunsinane

2. Design and make puppets. In making your puppets, refer to **Figure 1**. To make your puppet talk, insert your hand into the bag and curl your fingers so the upper face on the top of the bag moves up and down.

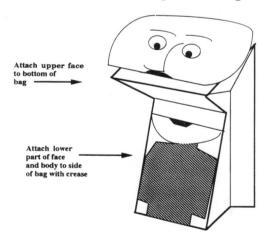

Attach upper face to bottom of bag →

Attach lower part of face and body to side of bag with crease →

Figure 1
Paper Bag Puppet

3. Prepare your script as if you were doing an oral interpretation. See specific directions entitled "Extending Activity for *Macbeth:* Oral Interpretation."

4. Decide how you can make your puppet walk and move.

5. Practice, practice, practice.

NAME:_____   DATE:_____

Extending Activity
for
Macbeth
Paper Plate Masks

Directions: One way to help you present scenes from *Macbeth* is to create a half mask to represent the character in a specific scene. When you present your scene, hold the mask in front of you to create the character.

large white paper plates (do not use plastic plates)
large craft stick
scissors
glue (either rubber cement or hot melt glue gun work well)
assorted construction paper, ribbon, cloth, cardboard, yarn to make hair, hats and other decorations that help represent the character
crayons, colored pencils, or felt-tip markers

Assemble the mask as illustrated in **Figure 2.**

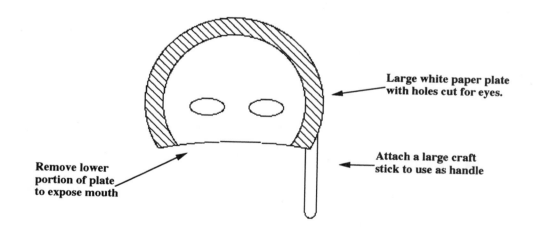

Large white paper plate with holes cut for eyes.

Remove lower portion of plate to expose mouth

Attach a large craft stick to use as handle

Figure 2
Paper Plate Mask

You may want to draw or paint on the plate or use construction paper directly.

NAME:_____   DATE:_____

Extending Activities
for
Macbeth
Writing Assignments

Directions: Presented below are some ideas for possible writing assignments based on your understanding of the characters and situations in *Macbeth*.

1. You are the casting director for a new rock version of *Macbeth*. Write a letter to the film's producers explaining which current film, television, or rock and roll stars you would like to cast in each of the play's principal roles: Macbeth, Lady Macbeth, Banquo, Duncan, Malcolm, and Macduff.

2. Write Lady Macbeth's letter of farewell to her husband before she kills herself.

3. Write a new or more satisfying ending to the play.

4. Create a "Meeting of Minds" where characters from *Macbeth* interact with characters from other works of literature. You may also want to have the characters interact with their authors.

5. Create a children's version of the play. Check *Shake Hands with Shakespeare* or Charles and Caroline Lamb's *Tales from Shakespeare.*

6. Create an illustrated children's book based upon *Macbeth.*

7. Write Malcolm's eulogy for his father, King Duncan.

8. Investigate the Globe Theater restoration project in London and report your findings to the class.

9. Research the food, clothing, housing, festivals, or celebrations for either Elizabethan England or Scotland during the time of Macbeth (approximately 1100 A.D.).

10. Using the character diary that you kept during your reading of the play, write a letter to your cousin in London relaying both the events of the play and your response to them.

11. As one of the characters in the play, write a letter to either "Dear Abby" or "Ann Landers" and imagine the columnist's reply.

12. Research the development and historical aspect of weapons used at the time of *Macbeth* (approximately 1200 A.D.) or in Shakespeare's time (1600 A.D.).

PART THREE

Appendices

Appendix A

EVALUATING READING PROCESS ACTIVITIES

This section serves three purposes:

- ❧ to suggest means to incorporate the evaluation of reading process activities into a grade for a unit on *Macbeth:*
- ❧ to explain how to set up and review reading activity folders;
- ❧ to review the instructional goals for the activities in this resource and to suggest specific guidelines for evaluating them.

ASSESSING STUDENTS' PARTICIPATION

With a reading workshop approach to literature, just as with a writing workshop approach to written composition, you must decide how to assess the students' participation in process activities and to evaluate the formal products that demonstrate learning as well. The activities in this resource provide opportunities for students to improve their reading, writing, speaking, listening, and critical thinking processes as well as learn about *Macbeth*. Although you don't need to grade all the process activities formally, you will want to review and respond to your students' work as they read the play. If you and your students were to devote approximately three weeks to a unit on *Macbeth,* you might use the percentages listed in the table below.

SUGGESTED COMPONENTS OF UNIT GRADE

Activity	*Percentage of Unit Grade*	*Numbers of Items and Point Values*	*Total*
Prereading activities	8%	(8 reading sessions @ 5 pts.)	40 pts.
Response journals or character diaries	25%	(5 [one per act] @ 25 pts.)	125 pts.
Postreading activities	10%	(5 summary sessions @ 10 pts.)	50 pts.
Comprehension checks	10%	(5 @ 10 pts.)	50 pts.
Vocabulary review quizzes	10%	(5 @ 10 pts.)	50 pts.
Language exploration activities	10%	(5 @ 10 pts.)	50 pts.
Language exploration review quiz	2%		10 pts.
Individual or group extending activity	25%		125 pts.
Total	**100%**		**500 pts.**

SETTING UP AND REVIEWING READING ACTIVITY FOLDERS

Reading folders allow the students to keep their prereading, during-reading, and postreading activities together for the entire unit. Any type of folder works well although two pocket folders allow students to store their response journals or character diaries on one side and other reading process activities on the other.

To monitor the students' progress and to provide formative evaluation, review approximately 20 percent of the students' folders for each class period at the end of each day. Select the folders at random, so the class doesn't know when you will check any individual's work. Take a few minutes to skim and scan the work in each folder.

As you review each student's work, check to see that the student understands the directions and purpose of each activity. Use brief comments to praise the work specifically and to point out any deficiencies. Then record the date of your review and any point values. You might try using +✓ for outstanding work, ✓ for satisfactory work, and -✓ for less than satisfactory work because students may find these symbols less threatening than traditional letter grades. You can translate codes like these into a numerical equivalent for your records: for example, awarding 5 points for outstanding work, 4 for satisfactory, and 3 for less than satisfactory.

INSTRUCTIONAL GOALS AND EVALUATIVE GUIDELINES FOR SPECIFIC READING ACTIVITIES

This section states both the instructional goals for specific reading process activities and suggests means, if necessary, to assess them.

Focusing Activities

Although students complete only *one* focusing activity for a particular scene, all focusing activities share two common *instructional goals:*

- ❧ to organize student's prior knowledge related to *Macbeth;*
- ❧ to establish a purpose for reading a scene

Scenarios for Improvisation

Guidelines for Assessment:

Does the student

- ❧ actively participate as either actor or audience?
- ❧ provide logical motivations for characters' actions?
- ❧ establish actions that are consistent with setting and existing information about character?

Prereading Discussion Questions

Guidelines for Assessment:

Does the student

- ᴥ participate in discussion?
- ᴥ share ideas willingly?
- ᴥ allow others to share ideas?
- ᴥ provide explanation or support for ideas?
- ᴥ provide speculations that are consistent with the student's existing knowledge of *Macbeth?*

Speculation Journal

Guidelines for Assessment:

Does the student

- ᴥ address the issues contained in the question(s)?
- ᴥ provide explanation or support for ideas?
- ᴥ provide speculations that are consistent with the student's existing knowledge of *Macbeth?*

Introducing the Play with Videotape

Guidelines for Assessment:

Does the student

- ᴥ attempt to answer all questions?
- ᴥ address the issues in the prompt?
- ᴥ have an overall understanding of the scene and its conflict?

Vocabulary

Instructional Goals:

- ᴥ to review definitions of less familiar words
- ᴥ to demonstrate the effect of context upon meaning

Plot Summaries

Instructional Goals:

- ᴥ to establish an overview of each scene
- ᴥ to provide a reference for the student when Shakespeare's text seems incomprehensible

Response Journals

As one of two on-going writing-to-learn activities that students may use during their reading of *Macbeth,* the response journal has two *instructional goals:*

- 🐦 to summarize and reflect upon the meaning of the play
- 🐦 to recognize, record, and comment upon repeated elements found in the play, such as symbols, motifs, themes, character development, or figurative language

Guidelines for Assessment:

Does the student

- 🐦 record an entry for each reading session?
- 🐦 meet minimum length requirements for each entry?
- 🐦 respond emotionally, associatively, figuratively?
- 🐦 demonstrate an accurate understanding of the literary facts of *Macbeth*?
- 🐦 demonstrate an honest effort to begin making sense of the play and developing an understanding of it?
- 🐦 probe responses and attempt to understand them rather than summarize or paraphrase the action of the play?

Character Diary

As one of two on-going writing-to-learn activities that students may use during their reading of *Macbeth,* the character diary has two *instructional goals:*

- 🐦 to summarize and reflect upon the meaning of the play
- 🐦 to begin to evaluate the action of the play from the perspective of an individual character

Guidelines for Assessment:

Does the student

- 🐦 record an entry for each reading session?
- 🐦 meet minimum length requirements for each entry?
- 🐦 provide an account for how the character learns of the action of the scene(s) just read?
- 🐦 demonstrate an accurate understanding of the literary facts of *Macbeth*?
- 🐦 demonstrate an honest effort to begin making sense of the play and developing an understanding of it?
- 🐦 probe responses and attempt to understand them rather than summarize or paraphrase the action of the play?

Viewing a Scene on Videotape

Unlike using a scene to introduce *Macbeth,* viewing a scene after students have read it provides additional information that may help them to understand the text of the play.

Instructional Goals:

❧ to recognize that the performance of a scene affects the student's understanding, comprehension, and interpretation of it

❧ to compare and contrast a student's interpretation of a scene with the performers'

Guidelines for Assessment:

Does the student

❧ attempt to answer all questions?

❧ address the issues in the questions?

❧ demonstrate an honest effort to make sense of the presentation?

❧ begin to make connections between the videotaped presentation and the text of *Macbeth?*

Guides to Character Development

Although the students complete these activities after they've read each act, they will re-read and actively contemplate specific portions of the play. The students may examine Macbeth, Lady Macbeth, Banquo, or Macduff as major characters or Malcolm, Ross, or the witches as minor ones.

Instructional Goals:

❧ to recognize and identify means that Shakespeare uses to develop or reveal character

❧ to use evidence from the play to develop and support an interpretation of a character

Guidelines for Assessment:

Does the student

❧ attempt to answer all questions?

❧ address the issues in the questions?

❧ use information from the play to develop and support logical conclusions about the character(s)?

Comprehension Checks

Both the Comprehension Check and the Small Group Discussion Questions provide means for assessing student's reading comprehension.

Comprehension Checks (multiple choice)

Instructional Goal:

❧ to assess reading comprehension of an entire act through factual, interpretative, and evaluative questions

Guidelines for Assessment:

❧ answer keys appear in Appendix C

Small Group Discussion Questions

Instructional Goal:

❧ to assess reading comprehension of an entire act through factual, interpretative, and evaluative questions

Guidelines for Assessment:

Does the student

❧ attempt to answer all questions?
❧ address the issues in the questions?
❧ use information from the play to develop and support logical conclusions about the play?

Critical Thinking Questions

Instructional Goals:

❧ to connect the play to the student's life in meaningful ways
❧ to evaluate interpretations of the play using textual evidence, personal experience, and knowledge of related literature

Guidelines for Assessment:

Does the student

❧ attempt to answer both the exploration questions as well as the focus question?
❧ appropriately address the issues of each question?
❧ use specific information to support ideas?
❧ integrate personal experience, knowledge of related literature, and textual evidence?
❧ draw logical conclusions from existing evidence?

Language Exploration Activities

Instructional Goals:

- to review definitions of selected literary devices and examine them within the context of *Macbeth*
- to apply knowledge of literary devices with textual evidence to develop and evaluate interpretations of specific passages of *Macbeth*

Guidelines for Assessment:

Suggested answers appear in Appendix C.

Does the student

- complete the items that the teacher assigns?
- make an effort to apply the definition of the literary device to the lines in the play?
- review the passage within the broader context of the individual speech, scene, or play?
- provide specific support of interpretation(s)?

Language Exploration Review Quiz

Instructional Goal:

- to assess student's understanding of how specific literary devices affect the interpretation of specific passages from *Macbeth*

Guidelines for Assessment:

Suggested answers appear in Appendix C.

Has the student

- completed the preceding language exploration activities?

Vocabulary in Context

Instructional Goals:

- to review the additional meanings of words
- to analyze the use of specific words within the context of a particular passage
- to develop interpretations of specific passages using knowledge and context

Guidelines for Assessment:

Suggested answers appear in Appendix C.

Does the student

❧ complete the items that the teacher assigns?

❧ review the definitions of the words?

❧ make an effort to apply the meaning of the word to the lines in the play?

❧ review the passage within the broader context of the individual speech, scene, or play?

❧ provide specific support of interpretation(s)?

Vocabulary Review Quizzes

Instructional Goal:

❧ to assess the student's understanding of specific words in context.

Guidelines for Assessment:

Suggested answers appear in Appendix C.
Has the student

❧ reviewed the meaning of the words?

❧ completed the preceding vocabulary in context activities?

Individual or Group Extending Activities

Instructional Goals:

❧ to apply knowledge and understanding of *Macbeth* to new situations and contexts

❧ to provide additional opportunities for students to apply reading, writing, speaking, listening, viewing, and critical thinking skills

Guidelines for Assessment:

Does the student

❧ have a purpose and focus for the extending activity that is directly related to the play and the study of it?

❧ present information clearly and logically?

❧ present information, whether from the play or research, accurately and with appropriate documentation?

❧ present interpretations of characters or events that are consistent with the information in the text?

❧ meet all appropriate additional criteria and specifications that the teacher sets?

Appendix B

USING SMALL GROUPS SUCCESSFULLY

I advocate using small groups throughout this resource. Small groups are a great way to get lots of students involved quickly. Several practices that make these groups operate more effectively are:

- Assign students to specific groups. When they self-select their groups, they may socialize rather than focus on the task at hand.

- Mix students of different backgrounds, abilities, and talents. In discussion situations, multiple perspectives often lead to insights.

- Structure the group assignments and provide written directions (on the chalkboard, overhead projector, or on written handouts). When students know their audience and the purpose of the assignment, they tend to stay on task. All members of the group need to understand what their jobs are, what the final product needs to look like, and how much time they have to complete their tasks.

- Establish class rules for small group behavior and encourage students to work together.

- Monitor students' behavior as they work in groups. Move around the room randomly.

Appendix C

ANSWER KEYS
Comprehension Checks

Act I
1. C
2. B
3. C
4. A
5. B

Act II
1. C
2. E
3. B
4. D
5. E

Act III
1. A
2. C
3. B
4. C
5. A

Act IV
1. D
2. C
3. B
4. D
5. A

Act V
1. B
2. C
3. C
4. D
5. A

SUGGESTED ANSWERS TO SMALL GROUP DISCUSSION QUESTIONS

Act I

1. The Thane of Cawdor betrays Duncan by siding with the King of Norway. When Macbeth helps defeat the uprising, Duncan rewards Macbeth's valor with the additional title.

2. Immediately upon reading the letter, Lady Macbeth vows to urge her husband to overcome any barrier to becoming king.

3. The Prince of Cumberland was the title granted to the official heir to the throne. Although Duncan names Malcolm as heir, it isn't official until the investiture ceremony. If Malcolm has been invested, it puts another barrier in Macbeth's way to the throne.

4. At first she seems upset that she has little time to prepare, but then she realizes that this gives her the perfect opportunity to murder Duncan.

5. In Act I, Macbeth seems surprised that he might become king, but he seems willing to wait until fate makes him king. Lady Macbeth, however, is willing to do anything to help fulfill the prophecy.

Act II

1. Lady Macbeth sees to it that Duncan sleeps well after having plenty to eat and drink; she also drugs the wine of the guards outside Duncan's chamber. She also takes the bloody daggers from Macbeth, plants them on the guards, and smears the king's blood on the them, so that they'll appear guilty. When Macduff comes to escort the king, she urges her husband to look like he's been asleep. She also faints when she hears the news.

2. Lennox and Macduff have come to escort the king to the investiture ceremony. They arrive later than anticipated.

3. Macbeth finds he is unable to say amen to the guards' prayer. He also begins to hear the voice of his conscience saying "sleep no more."

4. Lennox reports of the strange storm during the night. Later Ross and the old man mention how Duncan's horses went wild that night too.

5. Macbeth's case is that the guards are asleep and drunk rather than on duty. He catches them with the weapons and covered with blood. Pointing them out as the obvious killers, he executes them immediately. When Malcolm and Donalbain decide to flee because they fear for their own lives, Macbeth suggests that they were responsible for hiring the guards.

Act III

1. Macbeth has convinced the killers that they have a grudge against Banquo rather than him.

2. Macbeth has become king, but if he murders Banquo and Fleance, he can prevent Banquo's heirs from becoming kings.

3. The murderers fail to kill Fleance, who escapes and makes it possible for Banquo's heirs to be kings.

4. Lady Macbeth tries to keep the banquet going normally. She doesn't want Macbeth to appear in any way weak because it could bring about another revolution.

5. That "blood will have blood." The murder of Duncan and Banquo will be avenged, and he will have to pay for his crimes.

Act IV

1. With the failure of his plot to murder Banquo's heir, Macbeth becomes desperate to know his future.

2. The first three visions make Macbeth seem invulnerable. He's warned to beware Macduff, but then the second prophecy says that "none of woman born shall harm Macbeth." That seems to apply to Macduff too. Macbeth sees the possibility of the Birnam Wood coming to the castle as an impossibility.

3. The fourth vision shows the line of kings that are descended from Banquo. It confirms that Macbeth will not have an heir.

4. Ordering the murder of Macduff's household shows how much of a tyrant Macbeth has become. He's willing to murder innocent women and children to have his revenge upon Macduff.

5. Malcolm needs to test Macduff's loyalty. Malcolm must be sure that Macduff will support him rather than try to set himself up as king once Macbeth is overthrown.

Act V

1. Lady Macbeth seems to review the major tyrannies of the play while she sleepwalks: the murder of Duncan, her speeches to encourage Macbeth to commit the murder, the murder of Macduff's family.

2. Malcolm's army uses branches from the trees to hide from the sentries on Macbeth's castle.

3. Lady Macbeth seems driven by the enormous guilt brought about by her actions, and those of her husband.

4. Macduff was born by Caesarean section and did not pass through the birth canal. As a result, Macduff was not "born of woman."

5. Macbeth interprets the prophecies literally rather than metaphorically.

SUGGESTED ANSWERS FOR LANGUAGE EXPLORATION ACTIVITIES

Act I: Simile and Metaphor

1. The simile compares the earth to water and the witches have vanished as easily as if they'd jumped into the water.

2. Macbeth's simile implies that the witches have melted like breath into the wind.

3. The simile compares Macbeth's two titles, Thane of Glamis and Thane of Cawdor, to the third prophecy: Macbeth shall become king.

4. Macbeth's metaphor implies that Ross and Angus' efforts are recorded in the record book of his memory, where he can review them.

5. Duncan's metaphor is that Macbeth is a tree or plant that he has put in his garden and will attend to faithfully.

6. Macbeth's metaphor sees Malcolm named as Duncan's heir a step to be stumbled upon or skipped over, as he climbs to position of king.

7. Duncan's metaphor suggests that the king is satisfied that he's rewarded Macbeth rightly.

8. Lady Macbeth's simile compares Macbeth's face to a book that is read easily.

9. Lady Macbeth's similes suggest that her husband should look like the welcoming host in his glance, his actions, and words while he prepares to betray Duncan.

10. Macbeth's simile suggests that the people throughout Scotland will grieve for the death of King Duncan.

Act II: Personification and Apostrophe

1. The personified Norwegian banners fan the people around the castle until they're cold. The sight of the Norwegians' flags flying above the castle frightens and chills the people.

2. The capital offenses have overthrown the former Thane of Cawdor.

3. Lady Macbeth's apostrophe addresses a personification of night.

4. The *martlet* (sparrow) is personified as building mansions and falling in love.

5. Hope of becoming king is personified here.

6. Banquo's apostrophe addresses the powers of good, such as angels or saints.

7. Macbeth's apostrophe is to the absent, sleeping king.

8. Again, Macbeth's apostrophe is to the now dead king.

9. Confusion and anarchy are personified here.

10. In Ross's description of the solar eclipse, the personified night (moon) strangles the sun.

Act III: Symbol

1. Although the King of Norway is referred to here as a symbol for the entire country, Macbeth is symbolized as the husband of Bellona, the Roman goddess of War.

2. As symbols of her power, the witch sails in a sieve which should sink, and boards the ship like a deformed rat.

3. The borrowed robes are symbolic of the title, Thane of Cawdor, that Macbeth does not yet own.

4. Lady Macbeth wishes to trade her ability to nurse children for the bitter gall that would feed the evil forces that enable her to murder.

5. Macbeth suggests that his wife's courage should be transferred only to males who can use it.

6. The dagger symbolizes Macbeth's desire to become king; once he grasps it, he then has the will to murder Duncan.

7. The symbol of the spilled blood of Duncan, the regicide, is so great that it would turn all the green seas red.

8. Both silver and gold are precious. Because Duncan is an old man, his skin is silver. However, Duncan's single most precious possession is his life, symbolized by his golden blood.

9. Macbeth's murder of Duncan disrupts the order of the universe; as a result of this disruption, even the king's horses become wild.

10. The snake symbolizes the coming opposition to Macbeth's usurpation of the throne.

Act IV: Imagery

1. Banquo mentions the witches' speeches and oracles; things that can be heard.

2. The snake can bite; the sense of touch.

3. Macbeth uses the imagery of night and darkness; sense of sight.

4. The first murderer appeals to sight in describing the sunset.

5. The imagery of feasting and food appeals to sight, smell, taste.

6. Macbeth addresses Banquo's ghost using imagery that appeals to sight and touch.

7. The images appeal to sight and sound.

8. Macduff's imagery appeals to sound principally.

9. Malcolm's images appeal to sight.

10. The tune appeals to hearing; like a ripe fruit, Macbeth can be shaken from the tree (touch and sight); the cheer (hearing); night (sight).

Act V: Irony

1. Duncan comments upon the placement of Macbeth's castle, with its sweet smelling air. What Duncan expects to be a pleasant place to celebrate is to become the site of his death.

2. Lady Macbeth's lines here work on two levels; one is that it is flattering to the king that nothing is trouble because they do it for him; the other is that this serves another purpose: that Macbeth and Lady Macbeth appear to welcome the king while they prepare to kill him.

3. Lady Macbeth's drugging of the guards has enlivened her.

4. Although Lady Macbeth is resolved to kill the king, she can't bring herself to kill him because he looks like her father.

5. Macbeth has just come from committing murder, a mortal sin, when the guards enter into prayers.

6. It's ironic that Macbeth murders Banquo to prevent the prophecy of his descendants becoming kings; however, Fleance, Banquo's heir, escapes.

7. Macbeth, who is now king and should be a servant of good, is recognized by the witch as "something wicked."

8. It seems as though all humankind would fall into being born of woman. In actuality, Macduff, being delivered by Caesarean section, wasn't born of woman in the traditional sense.

9. Macbeth believes it is impossible for the trees to march against the castle. The irony is that the soldiers camouflage themselves with branches, so it appears as though the forest is advancing.

10. Macduff reveals that he was born of Caesarean section, so Macbeth should be fearful of him.

LANGUAGE EXPLORATION REVIEW

1. B
2. C
3. D
4. D
5. E
6. A
7. E
8. B
9. A
10. E

SUGGESTED ANSWERS FOR VOCABULARY IN CONTEXT

With all these exercises, encourage students to discuss their ideas and interpretations, for their answers will vary. These are suggestions and should not be interpreted as the only valid responses.

Act I

1. The unfavorable state that Duncan refers to is the captain being wounded.
2. The battle is the *broil*.
3. According to the captain, Macbeth treated personal fortune with contempt; he fought unselfishly for his king and not for personal gain.
4. The Norwegians saw military advantage in a new attack.
5. The banners flying over the castle scorn the Scots who live around it.
6. Macbeth questions how the witches have come by their information that he is Thane of Glamis and Cawdor, as well as future king.
7. For Macbeth, the witches seemed mortal and earthly until they disappeared into the mist.
8. Macbeth volunteers to act as *harbinger,* the person that the royal train sends ahead to secure lodging. In this case, because Duncan has announced that he will spend the night at Macbeth's castle, Inverness, before going on to invest Malcolm as heir formally, Macbeth is quite literally a harbinger who must inform his wife of the king's approach.
9. The image of the witches as *weird sisters* connects them to fate, much like Scottish versions of the three fates of Greek mythology.
10. Lady Macbeth will talk her husband out of any excuse or barrier that keeps him from becoming king.

Act II

1. Here Banquo's image of heaven is thrifty; the heavens have put out their candles (stars) early. It's quite dark.
2. Banquo's *summons* is the duty that he will be the father of kings.
3. Banquo requests time to discuss the prophecies with Macbeth; however, Banquo's conscience is clear, for he owes no one special allegiance.
4. Macbeth sees the dagger as real.
5. The dagger leads and points the way to where Macbeth is already going: Duncan's chambers.
6. Lady Macbeth suggests that the guards are sleeping soundly from having eaten and drunk too much.
7. Lady Macbeth has also drugged the guards, so that death and nature can struggle around them and they won't awaken.

8. Lennox relates many strange events of the preceding night. Among them is the bird calling noisily all night.

9. The guards seem to wear the blood as badges, suggesting that Lennox seems to think that they are proud of what they've done.

10. The old man's *benison* is a benediction like, "God go with you," or "go in peace."

Act III

1. Banquo has seen two of the witches' prophecies come true for Macbeth: he's become both Thane of Cawdor and king. Banquo wonders how and when his decendents will become kings.

2. Banquo seems to be referring to the unbreakable obligations of his oath of fealty to King Macbeth in addition to his friendship with him.

3. Macbeth alludes to Duncan's sons telling lies about what happened to their father.

4. Macbeth refers to his successor, who will not be his son, but someone else with a collateral claim to the throne.

5. Macbeth presumably has proved to the murderers in an earlier scene that Banquo was the person who wronged them. As a result, they vow to kill him out of vengeance.

6. Lady Macbeth refers to ideas that have little foundation.

7. The image here is that the snake is only momentarily made harmless, not permanently.

8. Lady Macbeth urges her husband to smooth over his rugged looks.

9. The night will make people blind; it will also close their eyes.

10. Lady Macbeth urges her husband to play the jovial host, for the feast is not guaranteed to be festive unless the host makes it so as it happens.

Act IV

1. The apparition gives voice to Macbeth's fears.

2. The second apparition is more powerful than the first.

3. Macbeth feels safe, for no one can draft the forest into military service and make trees march on the castle.

4. Macbeth sees the vision as the beginning of a destructive force.

5. Macbeth seems to use *firstling* as first occurrence, and to suggest attacking Macduff's first-born (his heirs).

6. Ross urges Lady Macduff to inform herself that she lives in dangerous times and that she should fear for her life now that Macduff has fled to England.

7. Here the desolate shade would be *lonely* or *isolated* rather than *barren*.

8. Malcolm defines tyranny in terms of boundless *intemperance:* excessive indulgence without limits.

9. *Avarice,* as one of the seven deadly sins, is the excessive desire to gain and hoard wealth. The more Macbeth has, the more he wants.

10. Malcolm is convinced of Macduff's loyalty. He has no doubts.

Act V

1. The doctor recognizes Lady Macbeth's sleepwalking as having a mental cause.

2. The doctor sees that Lady Macbeth's heart, as the seat of her emotions, is overflowing.

3. Menteith suggests that both Malcolm and Macduff require revenge to the degree that it would excite even a dead man.

4. Lennox knows which members of the nobility are joining them.

5. Caithness suggests that Macbeth's cause is unjust and disordered, for Macbeth has no right to be king.

6. The small revolts that seem to occur on a minute by minute basis give rise to Macbeth's abuses of power as a reason to censure him.

7. Macbeth orders Seton to scour or search the countryside and hang all those who talk of his losing.

8. Macbeth would like the doctor to be able to obliterate Lady Macbeth's memories of their evil deeds.

9. Macbeth would like to have his wife's mind back to an originally pure state.

10. Macbeth recalls that once a scary story would have raised the hairs on his head, but now, because of his deeds, he's become accustomed to hearing screams of terror.

ANSWER KEYS FOR VOCABULARY REVIEW QUIZZES

Act I	Act II	Act III
1. D	1. C	1. D
2. E	2. B	2. B
3. A	3. A	3. A
4. B	4. A	4. C
5. C	5. D	5. C
6. D	6. E	6. D
7. A	7. C	7. D
8. B	8. B	8. B
9. C	9. A	9. C
10. C	10. B	10. B

Act IV	Act V
1. B	1. C
2. A	2. D
3. D	3. C
4. C	4. E
5. B	5. E
6. E	6. B
7. E	7. C
8. A	8. A
9. B	9. B
10. A	10. A

Appendix D

BIBLIOGRAPHY

Abcarian, Richard and Marvin Klotz, eds. *Literature: The Human Experience.* rev., shorter ed. New York: St. Martin's, 1984.

Allen, Grant and George C. Williamson. *Cities of Northern Italy: Verona, Padua, Bologna, and Ravenna.* Vol. 2. Boston: L. C. Page, 1906.

Barnet, Sylvan, Morton Berman, and William Burto, eds. *An Introduction to Literature: Fiction, Poetry, Drama.* Glenview: Scott, Foresman, 1989.

Bingham, Caroline. *The Kings and Queens of Scotland.* New York: Taplinger Publishing, 1976.

Bleich, David. *Readings and Feelings: A Guide to Subjective Criticism.* Urbana: National Council of Teachers of English, 1975.

Brockett, Oscar G. *History of the Theatre.* Boston: Allyn and Bacon, 1968.

Brown, Hazel and Brian Cambourne. *Read and Retell: A Strategy for the Whole-Language / Natural Learning Classroom.* Portsmouth: Heinemann, 1987.

Cambourne, Brian. *The Whole Story: Natural Learning and the Acquisition of Literacy in the Classroom.* New York: Ashton-Scholastic, 1989.

Christenbúry, Leila A. and Patricia P. Kelly. *Questioning: The Path to Critical Thinking.* ERIC/RCS Theory and Research into Practice (TRIP) Monograph Series. Urbana: NCTE, 1983.

Davis, James E. and Ronald E. Salomone, eds. *Teaching Shakespeare Today.* Urbana: NCTE, 1993.

Fox, Levi. *William Shakespeare: A Concise Life.* Norwich, England: Jerrold Printing, 1991.

Hamilton, Edith. *Mythology: Timeless Tales of Gods and Heroes.* New York: Mentor Books, 1942.

Lee, Charlotte and David Grote. *Theater: Preparation and Performance.* Glenview: Scott, Foresman, 1982.

Macbeth in *William Shakespeare: The Complete Works.* Charles Jasper Sisson, ed. New York: Harper & Row, 1953: 879–909.

McNeill, Peter and Ronald Nicholson, eds. *An Historical Atlas of Scotland c. 400—c. 1600.* St. Andrews: University of St. Andrews, 1975.

Miller, Bruce E. *Teaching the Art of Literature.* Urbana: National Council of Teachers of English, 1980.

Mizner, Arthur, ed. *Teaching Shakespeare: A Guide to the Teaching of Macbeth, Julius Caesar, The Merchant of Venice, Hamlet, Romeo and Juliet, A Midsummer Night's Dream, Othello, As You Like It, Twelfth Night, Richard II, Henry IV, Part One, The Tempest.* New York: The New American Library, Inc., 1969.

Muir, Ramsey. *Muir's Atlas of Ancient & Classical History.* 2nd. ed. New York: Barnes and Noble Inc., 1956.

Robinson, Randal. *Unlocking Shakespeare's Language.* ERIC/RCS Theory and Research into Practice (TRIP) Monograph Series. Urbana: NCTE, 1989.

Rygiel, Mary Ann. Shakespeare Among Schoolchildren: Approaches for the Secondary Classroom. Urbana: NCTE, 1992.

Stanford, Judith A. *Responding to Literature.* Mountain View: Mayfield Publishing, 1992.

Vaughn, Joseph L. and Thomas H. Estes. *Reading and Reasoning Beyond the Primary Grades.* Boston: Allyn and Bacon, 1986.

Willek, Rene and Austin Warren. *Theory of Literature.* 3rd ed. New York: Harcourt, Brace & World, Inc., 1970.

Appendix E

VERSIONS OF *MACBETH* AVAILABLE ON VIDEOTAPE

Macbeth. (1971). Directed by Roman Polanski with Jon Finch. Color. 139 minutes.

Macbeth. (1988). Directed by Charles Warren with Michael Jayston and Barbara Leigh Hunt. Color. 110 minutes.

Macbeth. (1984). BBC/PBS production for "Shakespeare's Plays" series. Nicol Williamson and Jane Lapotaire. Color. 148 minutes.

Macbeth. (1987). Directed by Trevor Nunn with the Royal Shakespeare Company. Ian McKellen, Bob Peck, Judi Dench, and John Woodvine. Color. 150 minutes.

Availability and Cost

BBC/PBS versions are available generally through larger video rental chains, state or regional public libraries and educational film/media service libraries. Check with your school's librarian or media specialist.

Cost to purchase these video versions range from $25–$150. The entire BBC/PBS Shakespeare Series ranges between $2400–$3950.

In addition to video versions of the plays, check various sources for instructional films on Shakespeare, Elizabethan life, staging, the Globe Theater, interpretations of various plays, and dramatic theory.

Sources

The Writing Company issues a special Shakespeare Catalog. Address: 10200 Jefferson Boulevard, Culver City, CA 90232.

Filmic Archives, The Cinema Center, Botsford, CT 06404. (800) 366–1920.

Films for the Humanities & Sciences, P.O. Box 2053, Princeton, NJ 08543–2053. Orders: (800) 257–5126. Fax: (609) 275–3767.

Insight Media, 121 West 85th Street, New York, NY 10024. (212) 799–5309. Fax: (212) 799–5309.